FROME THROUGH TIME

Frome Bridge and the Blue House by Philip Crocker 1802

The cover illustrations are by the 19th-century artist WW Wheatley and reproduced by kind permission of Steve Horler and Garfield Austin. The front shows the porch of the Old Nunnery at Keyford in the 1840s, and the rear a watercolour of the cottages at Gorehedge c1850.

FROME THROUGH TIME

a popular guide to the town's history

MICK DAVIS

THE HOBNOB PRESS
in conjunction with the
FROME SOCIETY FOR LOCAL STUDY

Dedicated to my wife Lorraine without whose forbearance this would never have seen the light of day.

First published in the United Kingdom in 2023

by The Hobnob Press,
8 Lock Warehouse, Severn Road, Gloucester GL1 2GA
www.hobnobpress.co.uk
in conjunction with the Frome Society for Local Study

© Mick Davis 2023

Mick Davis hereby asserts his moral rights to be identified as the author of the Work.

All rights reserved. No part of this publication may be reproduced, stored in a retrieval system, or transmitted in any form or by any means, electronic, mechanical, photocopying, recording or otherwise, without the prior permission of the publisher and copyright holder.

British Library Cataloguing in Publication Data
A catalogue record for this book is available from the British Library

ISBN 978-1-914407-62-8

Typeset in Adobe Garamond Pro 11/14 pt.
Typesetting and origination by John Chandler

CONTENTS

PLAN OF FROME 1774	10-11
INTRODUCTION	12
1. PREHISTORIC FROME	13
The Mesolithic or Middle Stone Age 9,000- 4,500 BC	13
The Bones of Stoke St Michael (Multi Period)	15
The Neolithic or New Stone Age 4,000 2,500 BC	16
Fromefield Long Barrow c.3500 BC	16
The Fromefield Stones	17
The Druid Stones at Orchardleigh	19
The Devil's Bed & Bolster	21
The Bronze Age 2,500-750 BC	22
Round Hill Tump	23
Jubilee Field	24
The Iron Age 750BC – 45 AD	25
Tedbury Camp, Great Elm	26
Wadbury Camp	26
Kingsdown Hillfort	27
Roddenbury Hillfort	28
The Nunney Hoard Discovered 1860	29
Coins of the Dobunni	30
2. THE ROMANS 43-410	31
The Roman Villa	31

Whatley Roman Villa, Nunney — 33
Blacklands, Hemington — 33
Upper Hayes Villa Wellow — 34
Mells Park, Leigh-on -Mendip — 35
St Algar's Farm, West Woodlands — 35
Pitt Mead Villa Sutton Veny — 37
Farleigh Hungerford Villa — 37
Paulton Villa — 37
Brixton Deverill Villa — 38

Other Indications of Rome — 38
Prescott's Head, Clink — 38
The Frome Hoard — 39
Coffin Spring Lane — 40
Roman Pottery Finds — 40

3. SAXON FROME 410-1066 — 41

500 The Aldefeld Francisca — 43
685 Aldhelm's Church — 45
800s The Saxon Cross at St John's — 48
934 The Witenagemot of King Athelstan — 49
955 King Eadred 923-393 — 50
1048 Rare Silver Penny — 51

4. MEDIEVAL 1066-1485 — 52

The Town Bridge and Crossing — 53
1086 The Domesday Book — 54
1086 Frome Market Place — 56
1235 Decline & Fall of Vallis Manor — 58
1300s Our Ancient Streets — 61
1477 Keyford Nunnery & the Sad End of Ankarette Twynyho — 63

5. EARLY MODERN 1500-1800 — 66

1500s Apple Alley, Frome's Oldest Street? — 66
1500s Gorehedge — 67
1525c Early Archway Vicarage Street — 69

1527 St John's Burgled	69
1540 Antiquary John Leland visits the Town	69
1568 Waggon & Horses, Gentle Street	70
1625 Plaguy house	74
1642-1660 Civil War Period	76
1660 The Black Boy, Wallbridge	77
1662 Joseph Glanvill Vicar & Demonologist	79
1667 Town Bridge Rebuilt	82
1668 The Fair Maids of Foxcote	83
1685 The Monmouth Rebellion	84
1691 The Blue Boar, 15 Market Place	86
1696 Iron Gates, King Street	88
1720s Lockups & Blind Houses	89
1720 The Blue House	92
1724 Daniel Defoe visits Froom	94
1726 The Weavers Riot	95
1746 Simpson's 'The Agreeable Historian'	96
1757 Food Riots	97
1757 The Turnpike Act	97
1763 Daniel Neale Frome's Highwayman	98
1767 Thomas Bunn:- A Frome Visionary Born	101
1770 Fleur de Luce Inn	102
1774 Frome Gets New Vicarage	105
1785 Jeremiah Cruse Survey	106
1785 Backsword: Men with Sticks	107
1792 Abraham Crocker starts his Press	109
1797 The Cutting of North Parade	110
1799 In Praise of Cyder	111

6. THE NINETEENTH CENTURY — 114

1803 Keyford Asylum Opens	114
1808 The Tremendous Storm	115
1809 George III Golden Jubilee	117
1810 The Cutting of Bath Street	118
1812 Vandalism at St John's	120
1813 Drunken Colliers Riot	121
1813 Jeremiah Cruse Map	122
1816 Potato Riot	123

1818 Assembly Room and Covered Market Opens — 123
1819 Cockey of Frome — 124
1821 New Shops on Frome Bridge — 124
1823 Broadcloth Weavers Strike — 125
1825 Frome National School, Bath Street — 126
1826 William Cobbett. 1763-1835 A Noble Agitator — 128
1827 The Notorious Howarth Brothers — 130
1830s The New Face of St John's — 133
1830 Unemployment in Frome — 133
1831 Emigration to Canada — 134
1831 Gas Lighting Comes to Frome — 134
1832 Reform Act, & Election Riots — 135
1838 Frome Workhouse Established — 141
1844 The Frome Literary Institution — 142
1840s WW Wheatley, Artist — 145
1840s The Infamous Maggs & Sparrow Gang — 146
1850 The Railway Station Opens — 148
1852 Madam Carlyle is Not Impressed — 150
1853 Rossetti School Opens (briefly) — 151
1856 Frome's First Police Force — 152
1861 Murder at Buckland Dinham — 153
1864 Skimmington Riding — 155
1873 A Bull Goes to Market — 157
1880 Mains Water Comes to Town — 158
1883 Frome's Skeleton Army — 159
1890 Recollections of Old Man Barter — 160

7. MODERN TIMES 1900-2000 — 162

1901 Motoring in Frome – the Achilles — 162
1905 Electricity Comes to Frome — 163
1914 The Refugee Crisis — 165
1917 Mass Labour Demonstration — 166
1918 How the George Lost its Porch — 167
1919 Frome Gets its Own Tank — 169
1923 The Great Fire of Cheap Street — 170
1925 The Frome Builders Strike — 171
1931 Buried at the Crossroads — 173
1931 The Skeleton Hat Box — 175

1932 Tragedy at Willow Vale — 176
1935 Mavis Tate MP - A Woman Ahead of her Time — 178
1939 Gaumont Cinema, Cork Street — 178
1942 Any Old Iron ? — 180
1945 VE Day — 181
1949 Scandal at the Abbey: A Dangerous Liaison. — 182
1958 Frome Society Founded — 184
1960s The Sack of Frome — 185
1966 Frome Museum Opens — 186
1968 Field Marshal Montgomery — 187
1968 Never Mind the Weather — 189
1978 Out of this World — 190
1987 When Joni came to Frome — 192
2009 Jenson Button – Man of Speed — 193
2017 Foo Fighters Hit Frome — 195

BIBLIOGRAPHY — 197

INDEX — 199

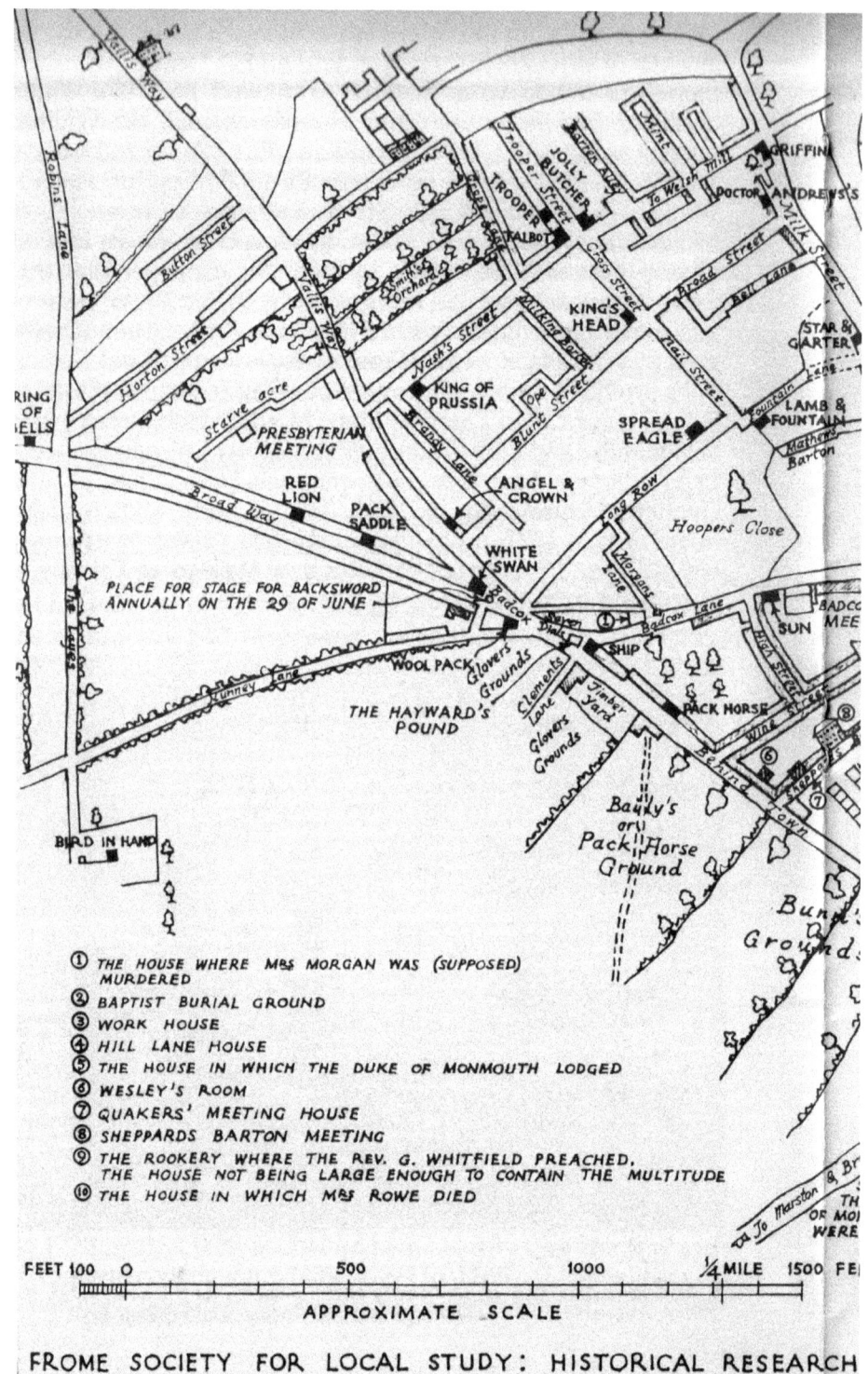

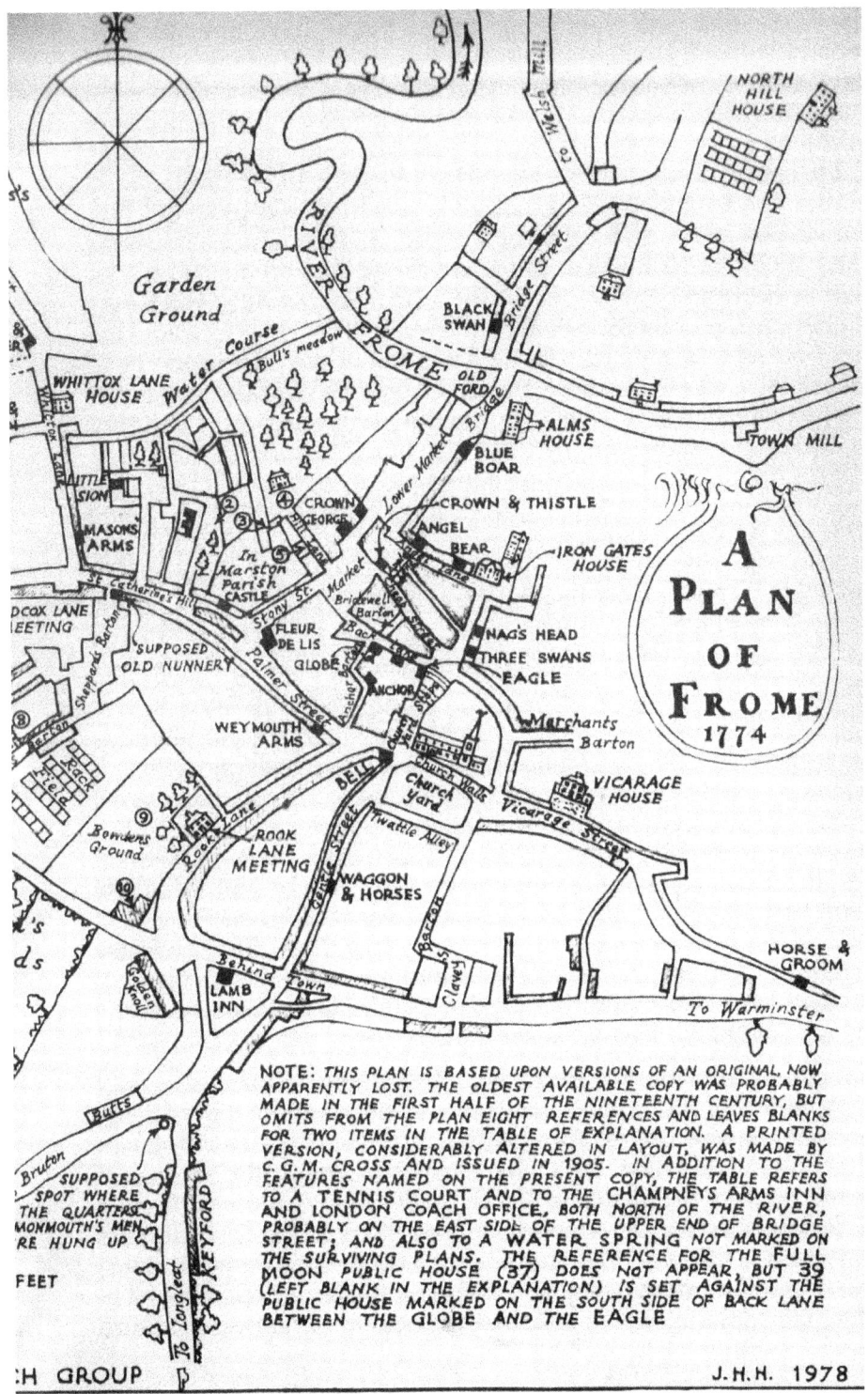

INTRODUCTION

There have been a number of histories of Frome notably, Peter Belham's *The Making of Frome* and Michael McGarvie's *Book of Frome*. The first appeared in 1973 and the second in 1980 before having its fifth reprint in 2013. Both are excellent contributions to the story of Frome but much research has taken place since their time and the growth of the internet has opened up a many new avenues of enquiry. With most of the early publications now out of print it was felt that a new publication with many more graphics might provide a suitable introduction to the town.

The book is arranged as chronologically as possible from the Stone Age to the Foo Fighters, but of course one entry may cover many periods, in which case the earliest known is used as the starting point. I have tried to find as many unpublished photographs and drawings as possible with many appearing here for the first time. Articles of greater length and detail can be found in the various publications of the Frome Society and the various research papers published in the *Frome Yearbook,* and there are a number of full-length books covering various aspects of the town listed in the bibliography. As well as a straightforward chronicle of events I have tried to produce a compendium peppered with a few outlandish characters and surprising facts. Occasionally an interesting story drags us out of town and off to one of the neighbouring villages as rich in history as the town itself.

The hope is that the articles included here will generate some interest and the stir the imagination of those perhaps new to the town or exploring its fascinating and varied history for the first time. There is a list of useful contact addresses at the back of the book.

Much of the research was carried out in conjunction with Frome historian and author David Lassman and some pieces have appeared in our joint column 'Frome Times Past', which has been a feature of the *Frome Times* since 2018, updated and edited where necessary. The rest of the material is gleaned from a large number of articles, publications, newspapers, my own researches and, of course, the invaluable internet.

Mick Davis October 2023

1
PREHISTORIC FROME

There is as yet no strong evidence of prehistoric settlement on the site of the later town but it is notoriously difficult for archaeologists to demonstrate a prehistoric presence in modern urban environments. In the case of Frome, there are certainly signs of prehistoric activity in the area but outside of the spectacular megalithic structures and burial mounds of the later prehistoric, evidence of 'stone age' activity is always hard to establish with any certainty.
It is fair to assume that the geographical situation which later people found attractive were present in previous periods and equally attractive. However, the inhabitants of the earliest period were largely nomadic and would have left little trace behind them. Previous historians have talked of important trackways through Selwood meeting at Spring Gardens and of fords across the river and the possibility of a settlement but as yet no practical investigation has taken place and no finds of an appropriate date recorded. What evidence there is of early prehistoric activity consists of chance finds as detailed below and involves exploring some of the surrounding villages. The dates given are of course merely an indication with cultures overlapping and evolving through time.

The Mesolithic or Middle Stone Age 10,000- 4,500 BC

The Mesolithic marks a period in which Britain was re-occupied by humans after their retreat from the intolerable cold of the Ice Age. Very little has survived from this period and many of these people lived and fished in rivers and ponds in the area now under the North Sea.

In Frome numerous flint artefacts have been discovered by amateur archaeologist Andrew Edwards mainly by field walking and sharp observation of ploughed fields in the Adderwell and Feltham Lane areas. As far as we know, being hunters and gatherers, their huts and shelters were slight and temporary, meaning that little survives. Mr Edwards believes that these ancient peoples

1 A selection of Mesolithic cores, flakes, scrapers, a small knife point and spear or arrow heads. (A. Edwards)

were attracted to the area by the river for fishing and the abundance of chert a fine grained sedimentary rock suitable for making tools and weapons.

Other sites from the same period exist at Easthill and Rodden and have been recognised by the Somerset County Archaeological Record since the mid 1980s.

The Bones of Stoke St Michael (Multi Period). (ST 66926 47558) (ST 6687 4745)
The caves known as Brownes' Hole and Stoke Lane Slocker lie near the village of Stoke St Michael five metres above the valley floor. There are two entrances to Brownes' Hole several metres apart, with passages leading back that interconnect and extend into a number of small galleries. Excavations by the Browne family of Frome in 1946-7 were extensive at both sites and amongst the reported finds were a human skull and faunal remains, including hyaena. Many of the finds are now in Frome Museum and associated material includes

2. Human tibia late. Iron Age (Frome Museum)

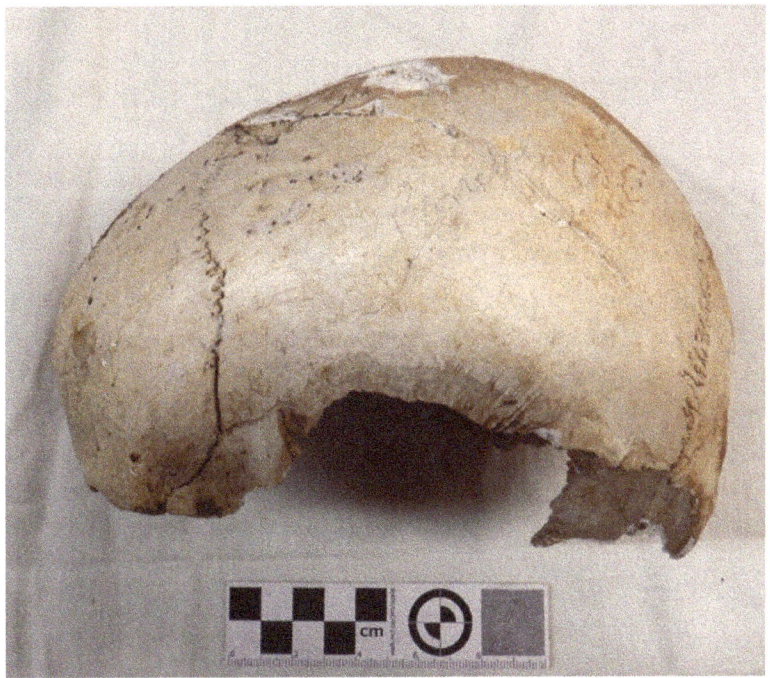

3. One of the skulls from Stoke Lane around 4,000 years old (A. Chamberlain)

bear, hyaena, red deer and wolf. The human remains date from the Bronze and Iron Ages with animal remains possibly millennia older. Cave entrances were known to be used as shelters and burial sites by the most ancient of humans.

The cave is known as Brownes' Hole (note the apostrophe) on the grounds that several members of the family were involved in the work. This is the spelling under which it is listed in the Mendip Cave Registry and other derived gazetteers. The Registrars are quite specific about details like this as they can be important in online literature searches.

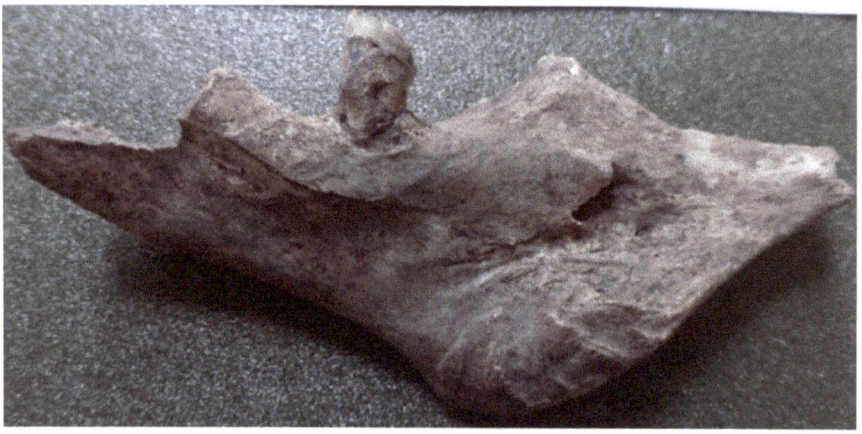

4 Part of a human jawbone from Browne's Hole (Frome Museum)

The Neolithic or New Stone Age. 4,000 2,500 BC

One of the most exciting periods in British, or indeed, world history must be the Neolithic, a time of great change and upheaval in all aspects of human activity. The change from mobile tribes or family groups that lived by hunting to settled communities and the domestication of animals. The west country is rich in remains from this period but the three sites described here are perhaps the best examples in our area.

The Fromefield Long Barrow c.3500 BC (ST 7808 4890) (FM 14103)
One of the saddest episodes in history of investigations into Frome's past is the complete obliteration of a Neolithic long barrow which survived almost complete until 1819. The Sheppard family of Fromefield House decided to level an unsightly mound in their back garden and discovered a series of stone chambers containing a number of skeletons which they claim they left undisturbed, (though how they levelled the burial chamber without disturbing

the remains is something of a puzzle.) A small piece of pottery was retained by one of the family at the time is now in the Somerset Heritage Centre.

There the matter rested until 1965 when a local builder was given permission to construct some houses on the site. The Ministry of Works were called in to conduct a 'rescue excavation' and discovered a chaotic jumble of stone and human bones from at least 16 individuals. The builder lost patience with the archaeologists when he discovered that he wasn't entitled to any form of compensation and closed the site down. He brought in his bulldozer, levelled the site, and erected what is now 14 Leystone Close.

The only records are a few photographs which are appallingly bad and the best of them is reproduced here for the first time. Some very sketchy provisional plans were produced. The file such as it is, is now stored at the Somerset Heritage Centre in Taunton and viewable on request.

There is slightly better news of the former inmates who also found their way to Taunton and reside there in a number of cardboard boxes. These were evaluated and assessed by Jackie McKinley of Wessex Archaeology in 2016. There was a mixture of individuals both adults and children totalling a minimum of 16 but nothing like complete skeletons which must have been disposed of by various gardeners over the years. The bones that remain could tell us a great deal about age, family relationships, and origins of these people were they to undergo scientific examination but that would require sizeable funds and laboratory availability.

5 A section across the barrow remains 1965

The Fromefield Stones. (ST 7817 4898)

A few hundred metres from the site of the barrow there are three standing stones long thought to be part of its construction displaced at a later date or even marking the sight of the barrow itself. An alternative, and more exciting possibility is that they once formed part of a Neolithic circle. Geophysical

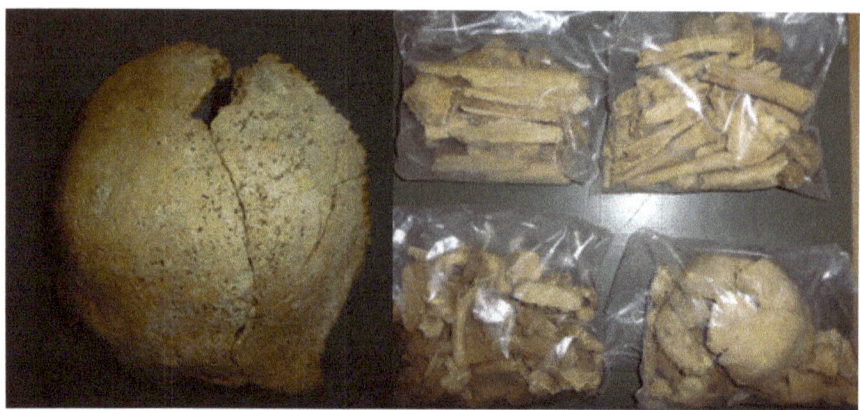

6 The remains of a skull and bone fragments from the Fromefield Barrow

survey results from surrounding gardens revealed the possibility of more buried stones and local memories supported the theory that there had been others. In 2016 an excavation led by Dr Jodie Lewis now of Bradford University and the present author put a trench down the side of the smaller stone but unfortunately the site had been dug over before and all we found was modern backfill probably dating from the 1970s. After much discussion the general conclusion was that the stones were probably boundary markers from around the 18th century. They stand on a former field edge which marks the boundary

7. The remaining stones at Fromefield

of a detached field assigned to the parish of Rodden surrounded by those of Frome. The stones were thought to be unusually square and overworked to be Neolithic, they did not appear on any maps going back to the 18th century there is no folklore about a stone circle and at least one of them had quite pronounced metal tool marks on it. The digging team was only available for one day and for the time being the stones retain their secrets. I have included them here because of a continuing debate about their purpose and origin due mainly to their proximity to the barrow site and the hope that they are Neolithic in origin. They are not. The full excavation report with maps and discussions can be found in the book, *Of Mounds & Men* by Mick Davis published by the Frome Society in 2020.

The Druid Stones at Orchardleigh. ST 76297 50667

Nothing to do with the Druids of course, who came much later, these two standing stones lie just off the road to the Orchardleigh golf course on Murtry Hill and are all that remains of another lost barrow described in the 1730s by John Strachey, the Somerset geologist and topographer as,

> Composed of small stones but turfed over. Some years ago viz about 1724 or 1725, taking away several loads to mend ye highway the workmen discovered the bones of a large man by several smaller skulls, lying in a sort of chest having

8. *John Skinner's sketch of 1819 Sepulchral stones at Orchardleigh; a vaulted Tumulus seems to have been removed from the site*

two great rude stones at head and feet, two side stones and a coverer. Some say a great number of bones. The barrow is ovall, has a pit or hollow in ye top and at ye east end are now remaining two upright stones about 3ft high which if opened might probably discover such another chest of skeletons.

One of the great antiquarians of the day, Rev John Skinner of Camerton made a number of sketches of the site finding it much as it is today. Skinner made the following note describing this visit,

…about 100 yards from the Murtre Farm House. This oval tumulus, for such it undoubtedly was measures about fifty feet in length, by thirty six in width being of an oval form, a stone being about ten feet and a half in height with another half that height leaning against it, still remain on the eastern extremity; a third has recently been broken in pieces. If the whole of this place of internment was vaulted similar to those at Stoney Littleton and Fairy Toot it would have contained a number of cists for internment but I cannot ascertain whether

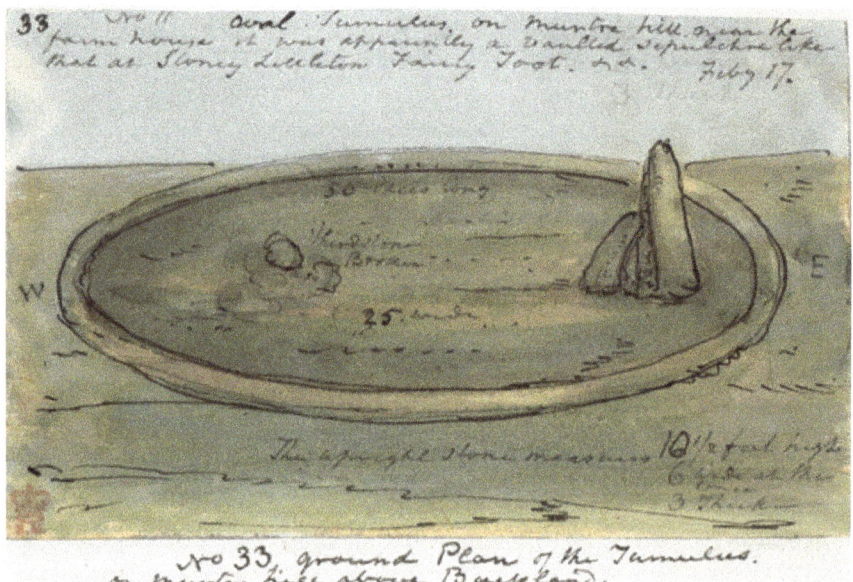

9. Two further views of the site drawn on 17 February 1825 (British Library)

10 The site today. (Jennie O'Kane)

this was actually the fact; indeed a person whom I afterwards questioned on the subject affirmed it was not the case; that he remembered it before Mr. Champneys moved the earth, but his description was so defective, I am inclined to think the earth and stones which constructed the tumulus had been previously removed before Mr. Champneys, had anything to do with it.

The upright stone is of the find of bastard freestone found near at hand, but that which has just been broken up and lies in fragments towards the centre of the oval is siliceous, whether this tumulus is to be attributed to the British or the Danes, is to me a matter of doubt; one of these days I should like to procure permission to examine the ground by the aid of the pickaxe and spade, as some record might be met with to elucidate the business, at present I must leave it in nearly the state I found it.

Archaeologist St. George Gray, excavated the site in the 1920s and recorded the mound as being 194 feet long 130 feet wide and 3 feet tall. He found the site to be a complete jumble as expected but recovered some human bone, small quantities of flint and pottery.

The Devil's Bed & Bolster. ST 8149 5333

About 700 metres from St. Lawrence church, Rode lies the scant remains of a barrow listed in Skinner's journal as, 'The remains of a circular cisted tumulus on Mr. Sheppard's land near Road'. He visited the site and made a

11. 1941 Looking West

disappointingly poor sketch of the area in 1819 with the caption, 'Demolished barrow which appears to have been vaulted like that at Stoney Littleton'.

Very little has been recorded about the site though field walking in 1977 and 1997 produced a number of flints and scrapers and Dr Jodie Lewis carried out a survey in 1998 which revealed over 30 stones some standing and some recumbent but she remarked that it was difficult to tell whether some of these were the result of farmers clearing fields. It has never been officially excavated.

The Bronze Age 2,500-750 BC

Towards the end of the third millennium BC things begin to change once more. The great long barrows were no longer constructed and the dead began to be contained in circular mounds surrounded by a ditch. Cremations became more frequent and the burial chambers were no longer left open. The trend continued with the round barrows becoming smaller and containing individual burials. How this change came about has been the subject of intense debate for decades but recent developments in DNA analysis indicate that over 99% of the gene pool was replaced with the arrival of people from the Rhine area. The incomers were known as the Beaker Folk after a type of pottery consisting of a large broad wasted drinking cup often found in their tombs. The area around

Norton Radstock is particularly rich in round barrows and amongst the most noticeable are,

Round Hill Tump ST 6900 5617
Easily the most impressive barrow in the Frome area standing about six metres tall and much overgrown but still dominating the surrounding countryside.

12. Round Hill Tump. Skinner's sketch of 1797

13 Round Hill in October 2015 over 200 years after Skinner's tunnel

First mentioned by the historian Collinson in 1791, Skinner first came across it six years later and in 1815 he employed two colliers who spent a week tunnelling into the centre only to find that someone had to beaten him to it by tunnelling down from the top many years before.

Jubilee Field ST 6889 5436
Jubilee Field is to the south of Radstock near a disused quarry at Fox Hills and is now a mound about two metres high and ten metres across, it was

14. *Jubilee Field Barrow, opened 25 September 1821 (Skinner)*

15 *The Barrow above Radstock in 2015*

opened by Rev Skinner on 25 September 1821. He describes the primary internment as a cremation in an oval stone cist just over two feet long and the same in width with a capstone six inches thick and containing charcoal and burnt bones including part of a cranium. Quantities of charcoal were found on the original turf line of the barrow which had a peristalith or revetment wall. It is still an impressive sight today on top of the hill overlooking the south of Radstock.

The Iron Age 750 BC- 45 AD

Hillforts developed in the Late Bronze and Early Iron Age, roughly at the start of the first millennium BC. The reason for their emergence in Britain, and their purpose, is the subject of much ongoing debate. It has been argued that they could have been military sites constructed in response to invasion from continental Europe, sites built by invaders, or a military reaction to social tensions caused by an increasing population and consequent pressure on agriculture. They probably served variety of purposes. We are very fortunate to have a number of them around the Frome area and four examples are set out below.

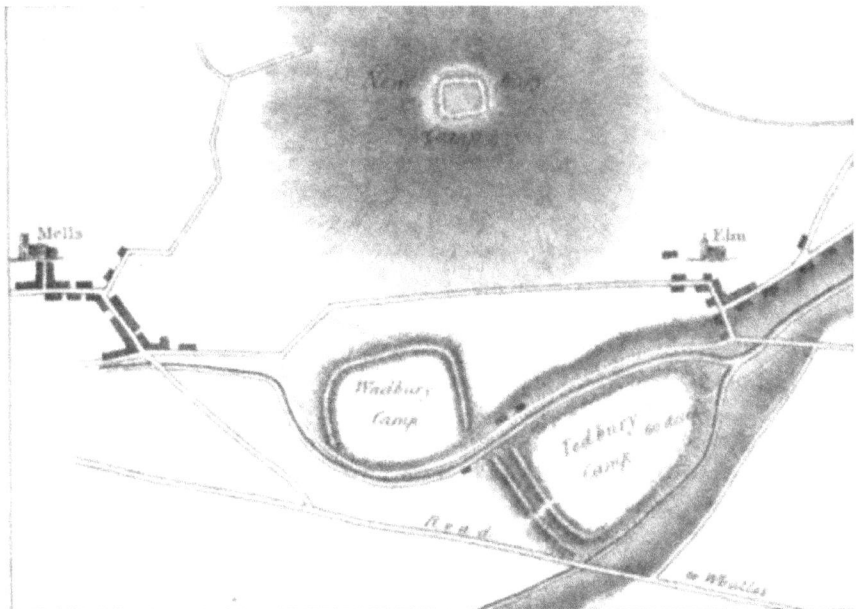

16 *The Three Hillforts near Mells*

Tedbury Camp, Great Elm (ST 744 488)
The inner bank varies from 1.2-1.8 metres wide and stands 3.0 - 4.6 metres high in places. There may have been a third bank. It covers an area of approximately 60 acres between the Mells River and Fordbury Water. The Romans seem to have occupied the site between 337 and 366 and a hoard of Constantine Junior coins were found in 1691. Further excavations and investigations of the site were carried out in the 19th and 20th centuries, with a quern, used to grind corn, being discovered in the early 1940s and now in Frome Museum. (FM1275). Being made of a solid hard stone querns, or parts of them, are hard to destroy and fragments have been found in Fromefield and Buckland Dinham.

17 The Tedbury Camp Quern (Frome Museum)

18 Tedbury Camp section through rampart (HER 23442)

Wadbury Camp ST 737 489
This earthwork would appear to be a companion to Tedbury Camp on the other side of the Mells Stream and guarding that river. It covers a total of about 74 acres and dates from between 800BC and the Roman invasion of 43AD. Along with Newbury fort to the north the three guarded the Avon and

19. Wadbury Hillfort (Google Maps)

Frome rivers, defending the roads and approaches to the mining district of the Mendip Hills long before the Roman Era.

Kingsdown Hillfort (ST 7188 5172)
A small Iron Age hillfort near Kilmersdon five miles from Frome now heavily ploughed out and covering an area of less than half an acre, the site was later used by the Romans. The site was excavated in 1927 and the few finds are now

20. Kingsdown Hillfort. (Google Earth)

in the Somerset Heritage Centre. The surviving bank is only about a metre high in places and around ten metres wide. The tenant farmer did not know of its existence and had driven a water pipe line through it in recent years, which exposed part of a large buried ditch in section.

Roddenbury Hillfort ST 8628 3757

Roddenbury Hillfort occupies a prominent hilltop about five miles from Frome. Only on the east side is the rampart and ditch well preserved. There is a short section of denuded rampart on the west almost obliterating the defences and elsewhere the fort has been destroyed by earth digging. On the east the defences are in good condition with the bank rising about five metres from the bottom of the ditch on the east. Today it forms a round-cornered triangle with one side facing the hilltop to the east and the other sides running around the natural contour behind, enclosing 0.84ha. The defences across the ridge are massive, with a bank up to 1.6m high and a ditch up to 1.8m deep below. Elsewhere the bank is up to half a metre high though absent in places, with a drop of about two metres to a broad terrace. On the north east there is a gap between the end of the ditch and the end of the terrace. On the south west the site has been disturbed by sand quarrying, probably during the 19th century. The entrance is on the east on top of the ridge, with a broad causeway over

21. The ditch and bank at Roddenbury (Sadgrove Creative Commons)

the ditch and a gap in the rampart, The interior of the fort, like the rest of the hill, is covered with shallow sand-digging hollows and now much obscured by trees.

The Nunney Hoard Discovered 1860.
On 15 October 1860 two farmworkers were ploughing a field near Horn Street in Nunney when their plough hit a small pottery vessel under a yew tree smashing it to pieces and revealing a large number of metal objects. The urn was beyond recovery and only a few small pieces survived but it was determined that it was round with an external diameter of about four and half inches and made of imperfectly burnt clay. The men had no idea what they had found but noticing that some of the objects were shiny they supposed that they must have some value and took a few into the village and sold them for pennies.

22. *A contemporary sketch of the find*

Once the word was out, others began to search on the site and one of these took two silver coins into a Mr Walker of Bath who recognised them as ancient British and proceeded immediately to Frome where the main part of the hoard had ended up. Coins were also offered to John Webb Singer of the foundry in Frome and to Mr Ballard a silversmith at 21 Bath Street in Frome. Walker gathered together what he could which totalled over 230 items and paid £16 for them. The exact number of coins will now never be known as they were spread around amongst many people and ended up in a number of private and museum collections but there were certainly over 250.

Walker handed what he had managed to recover over to the British Museum for examination where the vast majority were seen to date and from the Iron Age and had been produced by the local Dobunni people with a few early Roman coins mixed in. The British Museum decided to sell the collection despite its outstanding historical value and the majority ended up in the private collections of members of the Royal Numismatic Society. The hoard included what were possibly some of the earliest coins minted in Somerset bearing the name Antedragus of the Dobunni tribe and were quite probably buried at the time of the Roman invasion. The few Roman coins dated from the reign of the Emperor Claudius (41-54 AD)

About half a dozen of the coins are now in the Holburne Museum in Bath, some in the British Museum, some in the University Museum of Leeds and one silver coin is in the museum at Taunton. Although not as big or as valuable as the huge hoard found at Witham Friary in 2010 the find made a considerable contribution to our knowledge of late Iron Age coinage.

Coins of the Dobunni
In the late Iron Age, southern Britain saw the development of sites generally referred to as *oppida* (towns). An example of such a site has been recognised for some time at Bagendon, near Cirencester. The Dobunni lived in an area that today broadly coincides with Bristol, Gloucestershire and the north of Somerset, they were a large group of farmers and craftsmen, living in small villages concentrated in fertile valleys. Remnants of several fortified camps, or hillforts, thought to have been occupied by the Dobunni can be seen in the Bristol area at Maes Knoll, Clifton Down, Burwalls and Stokeleigh - all overlooking the Avon Gorge - and at Kingsweston Down and Blaise Castle.

Staters were the premium coin type of the Celtic culture, and first appeared in Britain around 150 BC. They are usually made from a mix of metals, predominantly gold (with silver and copper) and weigh on average between five to seven grams. Two or three iron age gold staters have been found near Frome, but are not well- provenanced (SMR 23562).

23. A silver coin of the Dobunni Tribe (Bryndlefly CC)

2
THE ROMANS 43 – 410 AD

It may seem strange to us now, living in the pleasantly situated town of Frome with its beautiful surroundings, that the Romans had little use for the immediate area. The site, lies at a crossing point and might have formed part of a number of possible routeways through Selwood, including the route from Poole to Bath. It had a fast-flowing river, a plentiful supply of building stone and timber, temperate climate an undulating landscape and good soil. Possibly it was too much hard work to chop into the great forest of Selwood which was probably infested by bands of marauding Brits. The Romans were certainly in the area, lead from the Mendip Hills was on its way to Rome within six years of the conquest making use of a British trackway and presumably improving it as a road on the way to the south coast, its exact route is yet to be determined and is the subject of much discussion. Maybe they were here – but little has been unearthed within the town itself all traces obliterated by the generations that came after.

The Roman Villa

Romano-British villas were extensive rural complexes of domestic, agricultural and occasionally industrial buildings that were constructed throughout the Roman period. They were high-status buildings, with hypocausts, architectural ornamentation and baths as common features independent of larger settlements, and found throughout lowland Britain and beyond. Some were simple farmhouses and others could be described as palaces, stone built with tiled roofs and mosaic floors, under-floor heating, wall plaster, glazed windows and cellars often with workshops, storage for agricultural produce and accommodation for farm labourers.

Some were undoubtedly built by the incoming settlers from the wider empire but others were built by the native elite often replacing or built alongside Iron Age farmsteads.

The building was typically arranged around a courtyard, surrounded by paddocks, pens, yards and features such as granaries, threshing floors, wells and hearths. There are a number in the area surrounding Frome, several partly excavated in the early 19th century by the Rev John Skinner and others.

24. Examples of the mosaic floors at Whatley

Whatley Roman Villa, Nunney. ST 74316 47005

A minor example is situated on a north facing slope overlooking the valley of the Egford Brook at Whatley Combe. It was discovered and partially excavated in 1837 with further investigations in 1848, 1958 and 1962 and was found to include a range of buildings around at least three sides of a central square courtyard. The southern range, partly excavated in the 19th century included a triclinium or dining room at the western end with a mosaic pavement with a bath suite at the east end. Trenches taken across the rooms of each range indicate that the villa was built in around 300 AD and partially destroyed in 350 AD but some form of occupation seems to have continued until around 370 AD. Finds included pottery, bronze spoons, a dolphin brooch, some coins and the skeletons of three children. To the south east of the main dwelling a semi-circular limestone spring basin was discovered with further buildings extending to the north. The site was left open and gradually eroded by the weather and souvenir hunters before its final destruction by a herd of cows.

Blacklands, Hemington ST 7652 5421

Seven kilometres to the north of Frome at Upper Row Farm lies Blacklands Field the site of archaeological investigation since the late 1990s carried out by the Bath & Counties Archaeological Society (BACAS). Although known primarily for its Roman remains, field walking and geophysical surveys have

25. Photogrammetry plan of Romano British Building 2003

shown signs of extensive activity dating back possibly as far as the late Bronze Age. The site has been much disturbed by modern ploughing and today little remains but the footings of the building but finds dating over a long period of time have been discovered.

During the 2005 season the remains of a large gatehouse were investigated assisted by Channel 4's Time Team and dated to between 70 and 120AD. A report on the excavations so far can be downloaded via the BACAS website, www.bacas.org.uk.

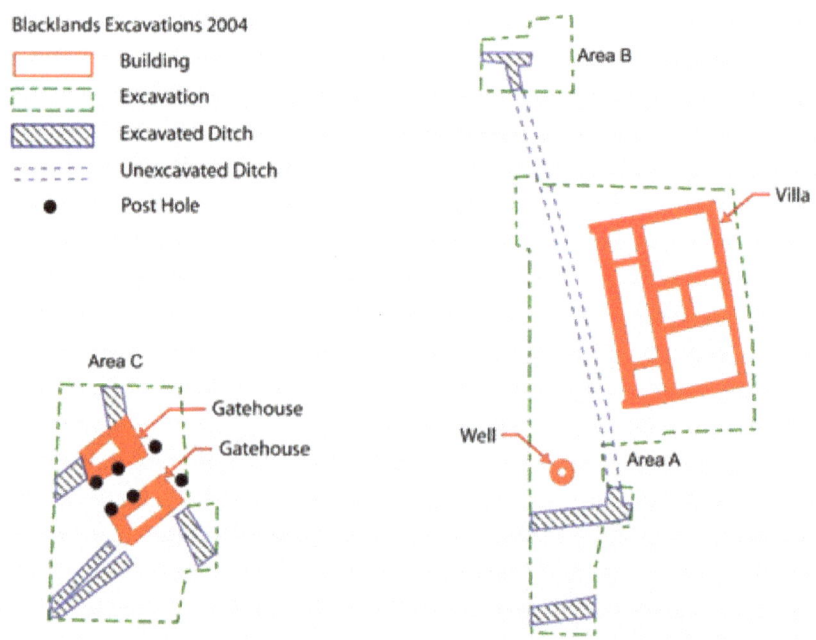

26. The Blacklands site in 2004 by kind permission of Jayne Lawes & BACAS

Upper Hayes Villa, Wellow ST 72812 57991

Described as a Roman pavement in a field called Wellow Hays this villa was first investigated by Aubrey in 1685 and again in 1807 by Colonel Leigh of Combe Hay 'for the satisfaction of his friends'. Sir Richard Colt-Hoare was there with Rev Skinner in 1815 when the soil was removed and a number of 'fine mosaic pavements' were

27. Pieces of Roman pottery & tessera retrieved from plough soil 2005. (English Heritage)

uncovered. (Archaeologia Vol 19 1821), but nothing has been discovered since. Skinner made a drawing of the building in 1822. (SHC - DD/HY/4/11/3)

Mells Park Villa, Leigh-on-Mendip. ST 70300 47500
Probable Roman villa identified from aerial photographs in Mells Park which seems to comprise a range of rooms and a courtyard facing east. The photographs show crop marks indicating linear ditches which may be associated. No excavation has yet taken place.

St Algar's Farm, West Woodlands. ST 78323 41854
Located on a gentle south-east facing slope above a tributary of the River Frome just south of West Woodlands is a minor Romano-British villa which occupies a low-lying but pronounced platform in the south-east quadrant. The villa is set within a roughly square ditched enclosure which survives as a buried feature, up to 1.5m deep, 2m wide and encloses an area of approximately 100m square. The site survives as entirely buried structures and deposits with no visible earthworks.

It appears likely that there were three periods of Romano-British occupation: an early villa in the 1st/2nd centuries, followed by a winged corridor villa in the 2nd/3rd centuries with internal room divisions, and an industrial site during the fourth century, possibly with occupation continuing into this period. A significant quantity of glass fragments, over 400, provides evidence that the site was also used for glass working; glass waste such as pulled threads and trails, misshapen molten waste glass, drops of glass and small broken chunks of glass, as well as crucible fragments were recovered in the vicinity of the villa building. Evidence for a furnace at the site has yet to be identified. Although no evidence has been found so far for walls or foundations to the villa, excavations have recovered building materials such as stone rubble, roof and floor tiles, flue tiles, tesserae, fragments of painted wall plaster and a cobbled surface interpreted as a yard. Metallic lead and waste material has also been found which suggests that silver was also being produced. Artefacts relating to the domestic occupation of the villa include a large quantity of oyster shell, animal bone, glass gaming counters, both imported and Roman-British pottery, coins and a copper brooch. There is also evidence of some non-Roman activity on the site shown by the presence of Iron Age and medieval pottery.

The buried remains of a possible mausoleum or shrine have been identified to the west of the villa, with a roadside settlement to the north and north-east.

A geophysical survey located a second square enclosure on the brow of the hill to the west of the villa which has the same orientation as the villa but is smaller in size, measuring some 40m across. The surrounding ditch, which is no longer visible on the surface, has a V-shaped profile, is 3m wide and some 1.5m deep. An excavation in 2011 uncovered its foundation walls and within the building were two human cremations. In an area to the north and north-east the survey located evidence for a possible Romano-British settlement. The area contains a number of pits, post holes and possible building foundations located parallel to a trackway or road that is orientated north-west to south-east, and continuing

28. *The Roman Pavement at Pitt Mead*

eastwards down the slope. Although there have been no excavations in this area the evidence suggests it is a focus of occupation and commercial activity.

Pitt Mead Villa Sutton Veny ST 90000 43300
About nine miles from Frome, near Warminster lies the site of two villas about 270 metres apart.

Although the published accounts (1785-1821) do not indicate a clear separation into two sites this is now thought to be the case. One was of winged corridor type. The western building had a probable bath suite and portion of tessellated pavement featuring an animal, possibly a hare, was taken to Longleat House as the land was owned by Lord Weymouth. These portions are now lost and the remainder destroyed, but it is thought to have contained Orpheus in a central medallion. Other finds include roofing tiles, painted wall plaster, brick flues, pottery, a coin of Claudius Gothicus with two inhumations. No remains of either building can now be seen but there are areas of disturbance in the eastern pasture and the western wood, probably the remains of earlier excavation and pottery sherds can sometimes be found amongst disturbed soil. The site was excavated in 1786 by Catherine Downes one of the first female antiquarians to excavate a Roman site. She reported her findings in a paper to the Society of Antiquaries in London in 1788.

Farleigh Hungerford Villa ST 7973 5830
This site lies about half a mile north of the village in Temple Field and is yet another site investigated by the Rev John Skinner in 1822 and partly excavated. It was examined again in the mid 19th century and found to be 114 feet by 33 feet containing a well and tessellated pavements. No plans or drawings are known to exist and there is now nothing to be seen. Coins of Tetricus, Magnentius and Constantine have been found in the area at various times.

Paulton Villa ST 67120 56740
Rev Skinner excavated in 1818 and discovered two adjacent villas approximately 130 x 70 feet adjacent to Chessils Field. One contained a large hypocaust and a room with a cement floor and painted plaster from the walls. There was a burial in one corner of the room and an urn with burnt bones. Traces of other buildings were found to the north and south. Coins of Pius and Faustina were found along with a trumpet brooch of possible second century date. Nothing is now visible but geophysical surveys by Ceri Lambdin and BACAS in 2002 have confirmed the site of the villa and the outline of some of the buildings.

Brixton Deverill Villa, Wiltshire ST 86145 38880

About ten miles to the south of Frome lies the remains of a villa provisionally dated to between 175 AD and 220AD, The site was first discovered in 2015 during the excavation of a cable trench and was subject to a small-scale excavation the same year revealing the remains of a substantial winged corridor villa facing onto a courtyard together with various additional buildings. Despite substantial robbing of the stone there appeared to be enough remaining to trace the outline of the building which appears to have been high status with an area of mosaic flooring hypocaust pilae and a possible plunge pool.

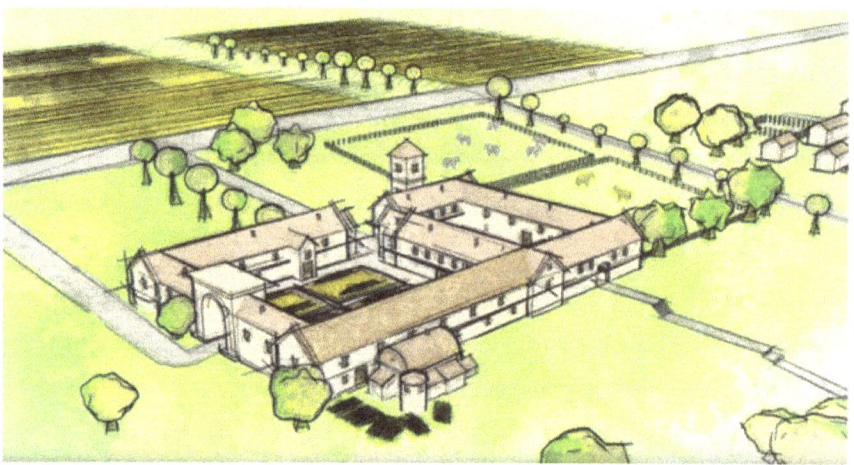

29 An Artists impression of the villa at Brixton Deverill

Other Indications of Rome

Prescott's Head, Clink ST 793 488

Towards the end of 1983 amateur archaeologist and police officer John Prescott was examining the groundworks connected with a new housing estate at Clink for evidence of the fabled 'lost Roman road', which is thought to have run from Bath to Poole. He soon noticed that one of the trenches for a new road had cut through a section of metalled track made up of pounded forest marble a local honey coloured stone much used for building about eleven feet in width. He cleaned up the section and took some photographs but could do little else as he was in the middle of an active building

30 Section through the Roman road at Clink

site. Prescott went on to examine the spoil heaps thrown up by the building works and discovered part of a carved stone head which he described as being 'on the site of a small spring'. This was examined by Stephen Bird of the Roman Bath Museum who concluded that,

31 The Roman Head

> It appears to be that of a full-cheeked youth, possibly a woman, and is inclined upwards and turned slightly to the right. It is broken off above the eyes and the surviving features are very worn and, in places, damaged. The features of the face show the work of a skilled craftsman…a lightly drilled pupil in the left eye suggests a date in the second century AD or later. Despite the wear and damage, it is clear that the head has been masterfully fashioned in limestone, perhaps by provincial sculptor fully conversant with the principles of classical sculpture…

A very rare and exciting find. Prescott claims that the head was sent to the museum in Taunton while he decided what to do with it and then it disappears without trace. The museum have no record of it having been deposited with them officially and it is likely that Prescott retrieved it and took it home. A full report on the find can be found in the Frome Yearbook 26 (2023) published by the Frome Society.

The Frome Hoard. ST 4300 41800

Amazingly, this was the third hoard of Roman coins to be found on the same site. In 1867 Charles Strickland, whilst carrying out drainage works at Quarry Hill Farm found 111 siliquae, or small thin silver coins produced in the fourth century along with a first century brooch now in the Ashmolean Museum, Oxford. The find lay under a flat stone about a foot beneath the surface along with some Roman pottery. Details of the find are unclear as no proper record was kept. The six remaining coins are now in the museum at Taunton. Some time before, Dave Crisp finder of the main hoard had found 62 silver siliquae spread over an area of 30 by 40 metres unassociated with a pot but probably once contained in a leather bag or purse and spread by ploughing.

32 A small selection of the 52,500 coins from Witham Friary. Buried around 293 AD

Coffin Spring Lane
McGarvie (1980) states that a Roman(?) stone coffin was discovered during the construction of Fromefield House in 1797. The builders left it by the roadside and for some years Spring Road was formally known as Coffin Spring Lane.

Roman Pottery Finds.
The Somerset Monument Record lists two finds of Romano-British pottery close to routes into Frome from the east, on Clink Road (SMR 23549) and at Styles Hill (SMR 24485).

33 The pot on display at Taunton Museum

3
SAXON FROME 410 – 1066

Little is known about Frome during the Saxon period, often referred to as the Dark Ages, and the first documentary record of a settlement in the area relates to the seventh-century foundation of a monastery by a monk named Aldhelm. The strategic advantages of the area, giving access to abundant natural resources, the Mendip Hills and Salisbury Plain, with their excellent grazing for sheep rearing must have been apparent for many centuries. It is known that Frome was a royal manor before the Norman invasion and that the town was on the edge of the great Forest of Selwood, *Coit Maur* or Great Wood as it was known to the natives, an ideal hunting ground and possibly the site of a royal residence. It is likely that the land had been in royal hands since before the time of Ine (698-726) Saxon King of Wessex. The hardy Saxon race were used to clearing forest and turning the land to cultivation from their own homeland in what is now Germany and the surrounding areas.

Though the Post-Roman and early Saxon periods were characterised by a return to non-urban lifestyles, the later Saxon period, from the 9th century onwards, saw the beginnings of a resurgence of trading sites and towns. In England this was controlled by the royal families and took place in the context of a network of royal estate administration centres which were already established. The reasons for the changes are complex, combining defensive, administrative and ecclesiastical considerations with increasing commercial activity. As one of the heartlands of the kings of Wessex, Somerset played an important part in the early re-urbanisation of the south, and there are a number of places which can claim to have been towns before the Norman Conquest.

According to the *Anglo Saxon Chronicle*, the Saxons first moved into our part of Somerset in AD 658. The entry reads: 'Cenwalh (King of Wessex) fought at Peonnum (Penselwood) with the Welsh (ie. the Celtic people of the South-West), and put them to flight to the Parret'. (the River Parret in West Somerset).

Nothing has yet been discovered to give an earlier date but there was a flourishing market and King Athelstan held a Witenagemot or great council here in 935. There are sporadic records of royal visits there in the 10th century which would imply that there was a town of some substance to have been chosen over several others nearby and that it was big enough to accommodate all the attendees and their retainers. There appears to have been a steady development of settlement in the Frome area throughout the Saxon period.

During this time Aldhelm and his group of monks, settled on a clearing by the edge of the great forest of Selwood near to a handy ford over the river Frome and close to the ancient tracks across the hill tops. This is where they were to found the monastery which was to become the town of Frome. Their task was to spread their version of Christianity and convert the Saxon peasantry. By the early 8th century, the Saxons were well established in the county, and the number of settlements began to grow. Evidence of established communities is limited, though throughout Somerset enough evidence has been uncovered to build a picture of families living in single farmsteads and small hamlets, surrounded by a network of roads of Roman origin which sometimes delineated the boundaries between estates. There is no reason to suppose that the area around Frome did not follow the same broad pattern.

It was during this period that the name Frome was first recorded, in a charter of 694. The word is thought to be derived from the Welsh or British name for a fair, fine or brisk river and is noted in a papal bull or charter of 701. If British in origin the name may pre-date the Saxon period by a considerable time. The settlement grew steadily in importance. It is known that the Frome estate was a royal possession by the late Saxon period, and may have been so from as early as the 7th century. The town was the head of the largest hundred in Somerset (and the wealthiest, according to the Geld Inquest of 1084), serving a vast hinterland of settlements in forest and marginal land.

The Domesday Book reveals that by 1086 Frome was thriving with a market and three mills, the title to the manor was held by the king and the forest of Selwood remained a royal hunting forest. The agricultural statistics in the Domesday Survey imply that by the end of the Saxon period, considerable clearance had taken place. There are other references from the late Saxon period to receipt of the 'third penny' (a tax on shire court profits) at Frome; and there may also have been a mint. Though all of these can be indicators of a burgeoning town, there is no indisputable evidence of borough status in this period, and no burgesses are recorded at Domesday. Nevertheless, there must have been a settlement of some size around the church and market though the location and extent of this remains largely unknown. By 1086 a number of secondary manors had been carved out of the Frome estate. Some of these were St John's (the minster estate), Rodden, Berkley, Marston (in which Spring Gardens was included until 1885), and two small manors at Keyford.

500 The Aldefeld Francisca
Spring Gardens, situated around a mile from the centre of Frome is a level area of meadow where the Frome and Mells rivers meet. The name was coined by the Sheppard family during the 19th century to make what was a wasteland of huge manufactories, mills, and dye houses sound more attractive.

Various historians over the years have remarked that this would have been an obvious place for an early settlement, and expressed surprise that no evidence has ever been found of one. It represented one of the best ways for travellers from the west to avoid having to scale the heights of the Mendips, and Peter Belham found no fewer than six ancient trackways converging at Spring Gardens in order to ford both the Frome and the Mells Brook. Back in Saxon times it would have been an ideal place for Saxon incomers to live and defend, being an open area of water meadow with rivers bounding the meadows to north-east and south-east, and high ground behind to the west.

Further weight was given to the idea of an early settlement here when we started research into our house, Marston Mill. We found that before being renamed Spring Gardens the area was called Oldfield. More importantly, a reference in a document known as the Cirencester Cartulary (a record of gifts to the Abbey of Cirencester) showed that the occupier in 1225, Richard Bigot, referred to it not as Oldfield but as *Aldefeld*. This is significant because both *Alde* and *Feld* are Saxon words, and Normans like the Bigots would certainly never have used a Saxon name for an area they lived in unless that area already carried that name.

Aldefeld in Old High German literally means 'An open area of ancient land used for pasture or cultivation', clear evidence that there must have been a Saxon settlement here well before Norman times. Initial research conducted with the help of Michael McGarvie showed that the mill attached to our house was a recent addition of 1750, and the original Aldefeld mill was sited on a bend in the river 200 yards to the north-east. Dendrochronology found that the new kitchen added to what must have been a Medieval Hall House had a beam dating back to 1508; and unusual green-and-orange glazed ridge tiles found near to the house confirm it was medieval house of high quality. This accords precisely with a passage written by Leland in 1544, stating, about 2 myles off I cam to a Botome, where there another Broke ran into Frome. And in this Botome dwell certain good clothiars havynge fayre Howsys and Tukkynge Myles.

But fine as it might have been our house is not old enough to have been lived in by Saxons, so with the assistance of BACAS (Bath and Counties Archaeological Society) we started to investigate our meadows. Geophysics revealed evidence of ancient plough lines and possible post-holes, and various test digs revealed numerous Mesolithic flint fragments and an unusual Mesolithic ball hammer (now both in Frome Museum.) Clearly itinerant travellers had been living here on and off for around 6000 years, but nothing revealed exactly when the Saxons arrived.

Then we had a stroke of luck. A chance encounter with an old acquaintance, Mike McGuinness, revealed he had recently taken up metal detecting, and so we invited him to investigate our land. Past metal detecting had reportedly yielded a Georgian silver spoon and a Roman coin, and Mike's initial investigation yielded a number of not-very-old coins, some slag, many horse and cow shoes, and huge numbers of nails and bits of other agricultural metalwork. To cut through the noise of these worthless bits of iron, he switched to investigating only non-ferrous signals, and after several days got a signal that suggested something big. After digging down some 19 inches, this turned out to be yet another large lump of iron, shown below.

34. Saxon Axe Head as found

Mike quickly recognised this as a rather important lump of iron, namely a Saxon Francisca Throwing Axe. What was so important about this find is that the design of Saxon Throwing Axes changed dramatically around 600 CE, and this axe design indicates a date no later than 450 to 500 CE. Below is a picture of the axe head after restoration.

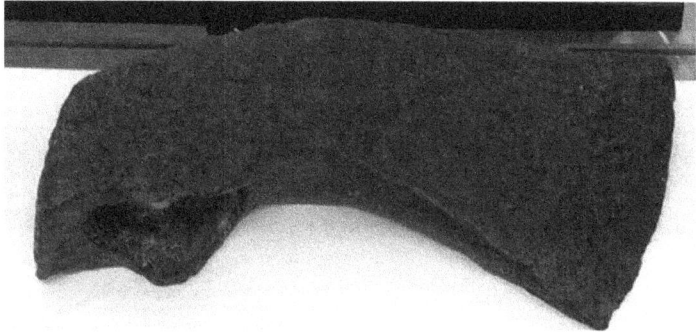

35. Restored Axe Head in Frome Museum

Conventional wisdom has it that the Saxons did not reach this far west until around 600 AD. Of course we cannot know when or how this axe ended up in our field, but Frome lies more-or-less on the boundary of the Hwicce, a tribe of Romano-British centred around Frome and Cirencester, who were known to have been hostile to the Saxons. It may have been thrown at the head of a Hwicce soldier seeking to evict the Saxon invaders from their settlement, or it may have been discarded after the party of Saxons had been living here for some time. After all, this design of axe, although very good for throwing at someone's head, wouldn't have been much use for cutting wood or hammering nails.

I think you'll agree that a sixth century design throwing axe in an area called Aldefeld is pretty strong evidence that Spring Gardens was where the Saxons first settled. And perhaps the Aldefeld Saxons or their offspring were the people who decided that Frome was the best place to build a church for St Aldhelm?

Dr. Robert Heath

685 AD Aldhelm's Church of St John The Baptist.
It is believed that St. John's Church was begun as a missionary outpost in the heart of the royal estate of Selwood, by the monk, Aldhelm of Malmesbury in around 685. He was possibly related to King Ine and cousin to King Cenwealli (643-672). Aldhelm was, by a number of contemporary accounts, a highly intelligent and educated man born in around 640. He became Bishop of Sherborne and was taught by the Irish teacher Maildubh at Malmesbury where he studied law, astronomy and mathematics. Aldhelm was well travelled having

spent time in France and Italy, skilled in Latin and wrote a book on the correct time to celebrate Easter, another on virginity and some poetry. He was noted as being a skilled performer in the harp, fiddle and pipes. It seems that he was prominent in a power struggle between two Christian factions, those supporting a Celtic version and those supporting Rome. Aldhelm was in the latter camp and ultimately victorious perhaps establishing his small religious foundation as a symbol of that victory. One is reluctant to use the words 'war lord' or 'chieftain' if only because no one else has, but it is hard to believe that victory was achieved by playing his harp and singing, as some pious accounts claim. The siting of Aldhelm's monastery /church is sometimes claimed to be an odd one, situated away from the more important river crossings which lay at Spring Gardens and on a north facing hillside. It is possible that the spring which flows through the site and into the leat which runs down Cheap Street, probably the oldest surviving street in the town, had some sacred significance that Aldhelm adopted, reusing an already sacred site to his own purposes and putting its water supply to good use, but this is speculation and it is just as likely that a good solid rock raised above the floodplain was thought fit for purpose.

36 St. Aldhelm as imagined in 1938. St Aldhelm's Church, Malmesbury.

Saint Aldhelm, as he became, died at Doulting in 709 and his body was carried from Sherborne to Malmesbury, a journey of over 60 miles which was broken up into stages with a special cross erected at each resting place. It is possible that the two pieces of Saxon sculpted stone set into the walls of the church tower at St John's are part of one of these crosses.

The date of construction of the ancient stone church remains undetermined, but there have been some exciting discoveries beneath the floor and a report on any dating evidence is eagerly awaited and it is hoped that further tests may reveal when it was built. The work during March and May 2021 revealed the south-west corner of earlier building contained within late 12th to late 13th or early 14th century nave. Perhaps further excavation will uncover even older remains and help to date the origins of our town.

Rev Colin Alsbury reports on the excavation,

Thanks to funding from the Culture Recovery Fund for Heritage we were able to ask Context One Heritage & Archaeology to investigate the areas below the timber flooring at the West End of St John the Baptist Parish Church in March. This work was undertaken as part of a feasibility study for the potential replacement of some of the timber flooring with a new stone floor in line with ideas suggested by the Diocesan Advisory Committee in relation to our reordering of the Welcome Area at the West End of the church.

Trial pits were opened up on each side of the Nave within the second bay from the West End. As was expected evidence of burials within the church was found – no graves were disturbed and any disarticulated remains encountered were reburied. Testing by a structural engineer found the ground to be quite soft with propensity to be unstable on the north side, though a little firmer on the south side. Discussions with our church architect and others have yielded the view that any future replacement of timber flooring by stone would need to be by means of installation of supporting beam structure rather than being supported by the potentially unstable earth floor.

A further pair of trial pits were opened near the centre of the nave close to the line at which the late 12th century building is believed to have ended. Substantial brick walled crypts with stone capping were found in the middle of the Nave. Evidence of robbed foundations in this area and some remnants of stone walling together with the evidence of instability at the west end allowed an extension of permissions to investigate and Context One returned in May to conduct further work funded by St John's Restoration Fund. The archaeological investigations discovered the west wall and long side walls of a building that pre-dated the late 12th century church. A significant linear disturbance immediately west of that line appears to indicate where

37 One of the Excavation trenches at St John's

the west end wall of the late 12th century church was removed during the extension of the church to its present size in the early 15th century.

A corner of walling on the south side of the Nave and related robbed foundations on the north side indicate the presence of a stone building exceeding 10 metres in length with an internal width of 4 metres, and with a slightly lower internal floor level than the later medieval church. This earlier building stood on the site prior to the late 12th century rebuilding work done under the direction of the Abbot of Cirencester, the then Rector.

These remains are consistent with being those described by William of Malmesbury in the early 12th century when he wrote of a stone church on the site larger than that at Bradford on Avon: "Stat ibi adhuc et vicit diuturnitate sua tot secula" – 'It stands there still surviving the centuries' [Anglia Sacra vol 2 pp7-8].

As yet the date of construction of that stone church remains undetermined but it is hoped that some samples awaiting radiocarbon dating may yield scientific evidence relating to its lifetime.

38 *The Saxon stones built into the wall of St. John's church*

800s The Saxon Cross at St John's.

These carved stones were discovered during considerable alterations at the church which took place in the 1860s and set into the interior wall of the tower but the circumstances of their discovery were not recorded. The top stone is probably the shaft of a cross, set sideways into the wall. The material is Bath Stone, and is probably 9th century and identified with the work of the West Saxon lacertine group. Lacertine consists of interlacing ribbons and animal forms. The shaft would have been set upright. A head of the dragon-like beast or *wyrm* is at the base as shown in the photo above, biting some interlacing, and the body intertwines upwards. A *wyrm* doesn't have wings, whereas a dragon does. The bottom stone is presumably a horse.

As regards any further survivals from the early period whatever there might have been was joyfully destroyed by Bennett in his rebuilding of 1852-1866. Local historian WE Daniel explained to a meeting of the Somerset Archaeological Society at Frome in 1911 that various early features were obliterated by Bennett. If the allegation is true, who knows what else he might have destroyed.

Address by Rev W E Daniel Rector of Horningsham.

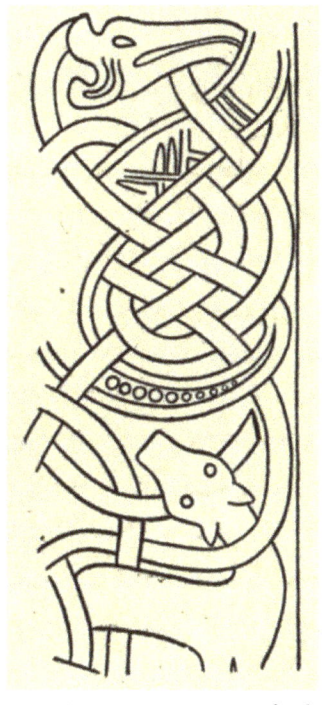

39 An interpretation of the carvings on the shaft (Browne 1903)

Under the tower of the Church were to be seen, carefully preserved, two ancient Saxon stones, and he supposed those were the only relics of that period remaining. There was a story, (though he did not know how far there was any foundation for it, that when that Church was being 'restored ') the workmen came across certain indications of an early burial which had the characteristics of a Saxon interment, and that the Rev. W. J. E. Bennett (who was then the Vicar of Frome), fearing that some antiquary would interfere, had them covered with quicklime. SANHS 1911 p.23

934 The Witenagemot of King Athelstan

King Athelstan held a Witenagemot or Anglo-Saxon council in Frome in December of 934 Such meetings were made up of a varying number of nobles, prelates, and influential officials and convened from time to time to advise the king on administrative and judicial matters.

40 A coin of Athelstan the Glorious 924-939AD

King Eadred. 923-955

King Eadred, whose name means 'weak in the feet', became king of the English and ruler of Wessex, the most powerful kingdom in the land, after his brother Edmund was murdered while defending his steward from a criminal who had returned from banishment in the year 946. At the time there was trouble and rebellion 'up north' and one of his first activities was to negotiate with the Northumbrian elite and to become accepted as their king. This went well initially but during the following year, his rule was opposed by the former king of Norway Eric Bloodaxe who managed to seize control.

Eric's reign was short as Eadred launched a destructive raid in Northumbria burning Ripon Minster and threatening the rebellious northerners with great devastation if they did not switch their allegiance back to him, which they did but not for long, as in 952 Eric was back again before being treacherously murdered two years later. The earls of that district restored some form of order under Eadred but it was not a particularly good period of history to be in power.

Little is known about Eadred's life, he didn't marry and spent most of his reign engaged in battle and maintaining his grip on power.

What we do know is that he died in Frome possibly after a visit to his friend and counsellor Dunstan, Abbot of Glastonbury on 23 November 955 at the age of 32 after a reign lasting nine and a half years. This information comes from the Anglo-Saxon Chronicle which gives no further details but a contemporary account describes how he was afflicted with a particularly unpleasant illness which meant that he was unable to swallow solids and sustained himself by sucking the juices out of his food. He was buried in Winchester and the mortuary chests in Winchester Cathedral purport to contain his bones. Scientists from Bristol University plan to examine the skeletal remains of the Saxon kings Eadred, Egbert and Ethelwulf using DNA

41 A Victorian, and possibly not very accurate, portrait of Eadred

techniques and a Heritage Lottery Fund grant has been applied to finance the project. Team leader Professor Mark Horton has stated that, 'The preliminary findings are very exciting.'

1048 Rare Silver Penny
A rare silver penny minted in early Frome nearly 1,000 years ago is now in the Somerset Heritage Centre was minted between 1048 and 1050 and measures just 15mm in diameter. The inscription on the coin reads BRINE ON FRO, Brithwine (Beorhtwine) of Frome.

It was found in Oxfordshire, and bought by the museum for £3,000. Assistant county museums officer Stephen Minnitt said: 'Coin production in the Anglo Saxon period was very different from today. There was just one denomination, the silver penny and each was individually struck by hand. Instead of a single mint supplying the country's needs, there were many mints, usually located in towns. Somerset had an unusual concentration'.

42 *The Frome Silver Penny from 1048*

4
MEDIEVAL 1066-1485

In Britain as on the continent, the medieval period saw the growth of towns and, to an extent, urban living, despite the bulk of the population continuing to live in villages. The reasons for this growth were many and complex. In England they included general factors - such as the growth of mercantile trade (especially the cloth trade) - and more specific ones - such as the post-Conquest establishment of a network of, theoretically, loyal magnates and prelates with large estates and commercial privileges. The latter led to the increasing relaxation of the royal stranglehold on the profits of towns and chartered boroughs (where tenants paid cash rents and were free of feudal ties), which in turn enabled the establishment of new purpose-built commercial areas (the majority of places classed as towns in the medieval period have at least some planned elements). Some boroughs were already in existence by the Conquest, and the existing pattern of Saxon urban or semi-urban centres was an important influence on the medieval one. This is evident in Somerset which, like many parts of the south and west (where the majority of the Saxon *burhs* and boroughs had been established), was peppered with small boroughs in the medieval period.

Frome during the late Saxon period was of both administrative and economic importance. It was the head of the largest and wealthiest hundred in Somerset, serving a vast hinterland of settlements in forest and marginal land: the agricultural statistics in the Domesday Survey imply that by the end of the Saxon period, considerable forest clearance had taken place. There was already a substantial market and mint and there must have been a settlement of some size around the church and market: the location and extent of this must remain largely unknown as once a prime habitable spot has been chosen people will stay there demolishing the old and building anew up to the present day. The lower parts of the Saxon and medieval settlement would have been subject to periodic flooding and still were until very recently. In the post-medieval period there was an elaborate system of channels and sluices controlling the water supply and drainage of the town, - the towns famed 'secret tunnels'!

The Town Bridge and Crossing

An earlier crossing of the River Frome during this time was by a ford which lay to the west of the later bridge and was probably in use since the prehistoric period. It was still in use in the early 19th century and clearly shown on the Jeremiah Cruse map of 1813. Although the river has had its course altered several times, it is possible that in the area of the ford and the bridge, artefacts associated with many centuries of use may survive awaiting investigation.

The first bridge was built in the medieval period, perhaps in the 14th century, when Briggehous (Bridge House) appears in the records of Egford manor in an apparent reference to Frome, although there is as yet no archaeological knowledge of it. Leland writing in the early 16th century, describes it as being built of stone and having five arches supported on a mid-river island, which also enabled the construction of houses in the post - medieval period. The bridge was rebuilt in the 16th century, but it was in the 18th century that it was widened and the first houses were built. The process was repeated in the early 19th century, when the present houses were built: the resulting scheme is now listed (SMR LB 26327, 26328, 26329, 26330). The central house, built on the island, was a fell-monger's, a dealer in hides or skins, particularly sheepskins, who might also prepare skins for tanning and in 1932

43 Frome Bridge from the Rear in the 1930s

it still retained in its cellars traces of the stone vats used for curing skins. It is not known whether any structural remains of the earlier bridges have survived the repeated remodelling.

1086 The Domesday Book.

Having defeated King Harold and conquered Britain William needed a comprehensive survey of his new lands which was compiled by 1086. Michael McGarvie explains,

> for all practical purposes it looks as if by the time of the Domesday Book the parish of St John the Baptist had already acquired those boundaries which it was to retain basically until after 1840. It was shaped like a somewhat battered and indented lozenge, except on the east where Rodden, itself a Domesday manor, plunged into its very heart surrounded on three sides by Frome. Frome parish stretched from Orchardleigh in the north, already in existence in 1086, to come down to an apex below Gare Hill in the south. On the east it was contained by the Wiltshire border and on the west by the ancient manors of Marston, Nunney, Whatley and Elm. St John's is one of the few churches to be mentioned in Domesday book by name.

The entry for Frome reads,

The king holds Frome. King Edward held it. It never paid geld, nor is it known to how many hides are there. (a hide was between 60 and 180 acres). There is land for 50 ploughs. In demesne (domain) there are three ploughs and

44 The Domesday Book of 1086

six coliberts, (freed slaves) and there are 31villeins (tenants) and 36 bordars (craftsmen, shepherds, labourers) with 40 ploughs. There are 24 swine and 93 sheep. There are three mills paying 25 shillings and a market paying 46 shillings and 8 pence there are 30 acres of meadow and 50 acres of pasture. Woodland, one league in length and the same in breath it pays £54.05 at 20 pence to the ounce. Of this manor the church of St John holds 8 ploughlands.

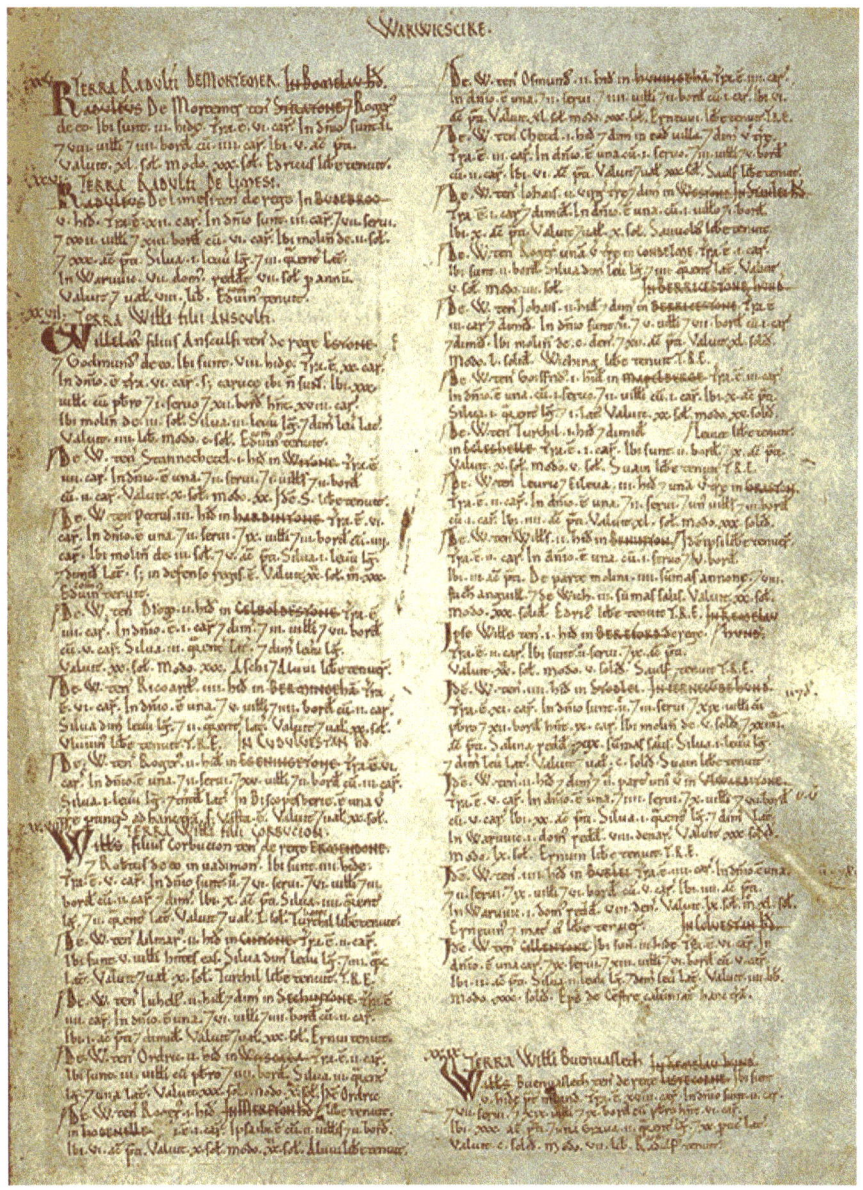

45 *A sample page from the Domesday Book, this entry is for Warwickshire.*

The commissioners listed 109 heads of household in Frome indicating a population of 400-500 and the overall impression is of a sizeable village for the time but without the prestige and royal connection that it once had although still a notable trade centre. Much woodland had been cleared since Aldhelm's time it seems most probable that the lands extended from St. John's down to the river. The entry concerning church lands states that, 'Reinbald holds the church of St. John'. He was a priest but much more than that, a favourite of Edward the Confessor, and may have held the office of chancellor becoming a very rich man being himself of Norman origin which enabled him to survive the transition to Norman rule. He retained his money and privilege under William who it can be assumed valued his counsel.

The years after the Conquest suffer from a lack of records or material remains and there is a sizable gap in our story. When Reinbald died, at unknown date, his vast estates passed to the crown and in 1133 Henry I founded Cirencester Abbey which he endowed it with all Reinbald's former lands making the abbot ruler of Frome. From the Conquest until the reign Henry VIII in 1509 the names of the priests are unknown.

1086 Frome Market Place.
There is no indication of the status that the town held in the Saxon period, it must have been of some size as there has been a market in Frome since at least 1086 when the land belonged to the crown which received 46 shillings and 8 pence in dues. In 1270 a Saturday market was granted and a three day fair given permission to take place on 8 September every year, 'for ever'. In 1494 there was a further grant of a market on Wednesdays which continues to this day and permission for two further fairs. Busy old place Frome in those days.

Until 1815 the market area had been divided into Upper and Lower halves separated by three buildings which included a pub and two shops and which stretched from roughly where the Boyle Cross stands at the end of Cheap Street and King Street to within few feet of the George Inn making

46 The divided Market Place in 1808

the street very narrow and inconvenient. These buildings were swept away in 1815 shortly after Bath Street was cut which widened the road and increased the main market area. The plot marked 27 on the map which dates from 1813 was an alehouse named the Crown & Thistle, plots 25 & 29 were, and still are, the George Hotel and plot 24 was yet another pub called the Crown, now Fat Face, a bizarrely named shop retailing wearing apparel.

47 Earliest known photograph of the Market Place, 1860s

In the top corner of the Upper Market place outside plots 32 & 33 lay the shambles or place where the animals were slaughtered and presumably this half was the part known as the 'beast market'. Adjoining the shambles was yet another pub the Anchor now the Garden Café. The photo is one of the earliest known and dates from before 1871 when the Boyle Cross and drinking fountain was erected. The market place was also home to the town stocks and pillory but their exact location is now lost.

The Great Reform Act of 1832 which gave votes to a few hundred local tradesmen and property owners was the catalyst for three days of rioting centered on the George during that year during which two people were shot and many injured.

In 1873 an act of Parliament allowed for the purchase, and improvements to be made, for a site known as Brownjohn's Mead bounded by the river, the railway line, Bridge Street and Justice Lane, the area now occupied by the Cheese & Grain carpark. Two years later the market moved onto this new site where it remained until moving out to Standerwick in 1990. The most recent improvements have included the removal of the pavement barriers and a reduction in some of the pavement widths so that the buses can pull in off the road returning the layout to pretty much how it was about 20 years before.

1235 The Decline & Fall of Vallis Manor.

One of the saddest episodes in Frome's architectural history was the progressive destruction of one of its most ancient buildings. The origins and history of Vallis Manor have proved very difficult to uncover. Historian Michael McGarvie traces its building to 1235 when it was said to have been constructed, or perhaps rebuilt, out of ten oaks given to a Ralph FitzBernard by King Henry III about three miles from the town. It is also probable that this is where King Edward I stayed during his visit to Frome on 14 September 1276.

The manor passed to the Leversedge family who became Lords of the Manor in the 1390s. There is a famous legend that in 1465 Edmund Leversedge, a proud, argumentative and unpleasant man was struck by a pestilence, possibly the plague, causing his face and tongue to turn as black as pitch and that he lay for a considerable time, (some say 40 days!) as if dead. During this episode, he had the most terrible dream during which he was taken down to Hell and given a guided tour. He awoke, so the legend goes, to find himself laid out for his burial, with his lamenting friends around his bier. The experience terrified him so much that once he recovered he became a reformed man. The Leversedge family embarked upon a major reconstruction of the manor in the 15th century and nothing still in existence by the early 1970s has been discovered that pre-dated that time. Whatever its origins the manor played a large part in the life of the town and its government pre-dates that time.

Disaster struck in 1606 when, as the result of a felony, possibly a murder, committed by Elizabeth Leversedge and three of her servants, the family had to sign away much of their land to obtain a pardon. The situation was not helped when they supported King Charles during the civil war and were twice heavily fined by Parliament. Later generations did not live at Vallis and the house was allowed to deteriorate with the magnificent parkland turned into a farm. One of their family, Lionel Seaman, who became vicar of Frome in 1742, built the vicarage near the church and lived there. The family had sold off parts of the estate over the years and what was left in 1751 was sold to the Earl of Cork and Orrery for £15,900 after an occupancy of eleven generations.

It seems that the house needed some repair but was still habitable. The earl had many debts which probably spoilt his plans for any grand restoration and he died in 1762. The great manor became a farm and has been so ever since.

Charting the decline of this once magnificent building is no easy task as it appears to have been friendless for centuries, possibly too far from town for the younger generation or too close to their other home at Marston. However, part of it was still occupied in the 19th century surviving as a carpenter's and wheelwrights' shop the beautifully made timber and stone roof still resisting all nature's assaults upon it. The Earls of Cork and Orrery presided over the estate's decline, selling off the remaining parts in 1905.

48 A view from the west in the 1860s showing the hall and private apartments

The building's roof was still largely intact in 1928 when Lord Hylton visited with architect Harold Brakspear who wrote,

> The hall retains its open timber roof of the 15th century divided by arched principles into five bays having a three purlins on each side supported by curved wind braces. It is covered with stone tiles which are now falling in.

Photographs taken in the mid to late 1950s show the magnificent medieval roof timbers still in place thanks largely to the survival of the stone tiles covering them but these soon went either stolen or sold on and with them all hope of survival. There was a concerted campaign by members of the Frome Society during the mid 1970s to try and save what was left of this important building. It was a depressing situation and in 1974 local historian Michael McGarvie was moved to state that,

> The great hall, alas, is beyond salvation'. It was probably Edmund's grandson William who died in 1485 who built the great hall. Even in the last stages of decay it is a spectacular and noble edifice. In it was originally of two stories and capped with a magnificent open timber roof of which one section survives in situ. Beneath the rafters were those serried lines of curved braces which are such a distinctive feature of mediaeval roofs. The principal rafters are also elegantly braced and the wall posts rest firmly on carved corbels. There are the remains of a cusped window and an arched stone fireplace. The gable of the chamber is still a striking feature and has an eight light mullioned and transomed window, (now blocked) of around 1600. Until recent months the great chamber have substantial remains of its mediaeval roof and we regret to say that this has now disappeared the whole structure is a significant example of a mediaeval manor house I know its development and adaption in the 16th century and later.

In October 1978 the remaining land and buildings were divided into lots and auctioned off but the final nail in the coffin was a letter from the Chief Inspector of Ancient Monuments which states,

> I have now seen the site and must confess that it really has gone too far and guardianship by Department is out of the question. The best thing I can suggest is encouraging the local

49 *The roof tiles start to fall 1959. (Roger Abbott)*

authority to take some form of limited stabilisation. We are hoping to meet to the council to discuss the possibilities but I am not optimistic of results. It is extraordinary that this building was not appreciated in the past with something might have been done to save it.

c1300 Our Ancient Streets.

50 Gentle Street in 2016

Frome Market Place was, as we have seen, firmly in existence by 1086 by which time Aldhelm's church had been around in some form or other for around 400 years. A church would serve little purpose without a population to support it and so pathways from the river and the market would have wended their way toward it as cottages, workshops and small traders grew up along the paths.

Gentle Street, once known as Hunger Lane, Old English for 'land on a steep slope' which it most certainly is, was first recorded in 1300 and joins on to what is now King Street from market place to church. The meeting point between the two, running along the churchyard wall is now a set of wide stone steps but was once Church Slope and is also mentioned in around 1300 Vicarage Street appears as Vicarestret as early as 1392 and Cheap Street the

51 The Jeremiah Cruse map of 1813

oldest trading street with its leat of water running down from the church along the middle until it disappears underground and off to the river.

The street marked as New Road to the left of the 1813 map is now Bath Street which was not cut until after 1810 to provide an easier and direct route out of town which before could only be achieved by negotiating the narrow and treacherous lanes of Stony Street first mentioned by name in 1568 or Palmer Street and through a maze of tenements known as Anchor Barton after a pub that stood there.

There may even have been an ancient village now long vanished named Pikewell and standing somewhere near Spring Gardens with its own church but references are slight and nothing has yet been discovered of its location.

Outside of the town centre there is the town bridge very probably a fording point of some sort during Aldhelm's time or many years before.

1477 Keyford Nunnery & the Sad End of Ankarette Twynyho.
One of Frome's most intriguing buildings lies at Lower Keyford just off Culver Hill and known locally as Keyford Nunnery. Information is patchy but it is believed that once formed the home of the Twynyho family and dated originally from the early 15th century. There is no record of a nunnery having existed in this location but the name is of longstanding, Monmouth is said to have stabled his horses at 'The Old Nunnery House' during his campaign of 1685. When the historian John Strachey saw it in 1740 it was already in poor repair. The story begins with Isabel Neville, daughter of Richard Neville, Earl of Warwick, whose machinations led to the disposition of two kings and epithet of 'Kingmaker'. In 1469, Isabel married George Plantagenet, the Duke of Clarence and brother of Edward IV, and by 1476 she had given birth to a son, Edward, and daughter, Margaret. The Duchess of Clarence, as Isabel was known, produced another son, Richard, in October 1476, but two months later, on 22 December, she died at Warwick Castle.

Although it is now widely believed that her death was a result of either consumption or childbed fever, the Duke of Clarence concluded that his wife had been poisoned. A suspect was sought, and the blame fell upon one of the Duchess's former lady-attendants, Ankarette Twynyho. Ankarette was the widow of William Twynyho of Keyford – a prominent family in the area – and lived at the Old Nunnery, at the bottom of Culver Hill. During the afternoon of 12 April 1477, and on the orders of Clarence, around two dozen men burst into her residence and unlawfully seized Ankarette, 'with great violence'.

52 The house in 1827 by which time it had become notorious as the home of the Howarth family of burglars, every corner crammed with the stolen loot of many years.

They arrived at Warwick, along with their victim, on Monday, having spent the previous two evenings of their journey in Bath and Gloucester. The following day she was brought before the Duke and charged that on 10 October she had given his deceased wife 'a venomous drink of ale mixed with poison.'

Ankarette protested her innocence but to no avail; the jury condemned her, and she was taken away to nearby gallows and hanged within three hours. Before her execution, however, many of the jurors came to her to ask forgiveness, declaring they had given their verdict under compulsion and in fear of their lives. Did the Duchess of Clarence die of natural causes, as is widely believed today, or was she poisoned, as her husband claimed?

Whatever the cause it seems that Ankarette was innocent, but if the duchess's death was by another hand, who did administer the 'venomous mix'?

In a surprising twist, strong suspicion rests on Clarence himself, as at the time of his wife's death, his matrimonial eyes were already elsewhere. This was in the direction of Mary, daughter and heiress of the Duke of Burgundy, whose hand in marriage would be a 'great prize' to the successful suitor. Whatever the truth, the Duke of Clarence failed in his scheme, as Mary married her first love, the Emperor Maximillian. But this was not the end of the story. Clarence was himself executed, around ten months later, after a plot against his brother, the king, was uncovered and his part within it discovered and later that same year Ankarette was posthumously pardoned by Edward IV, after a petition was submitted by her nephew, Roger Twynyho.

53 The Home of Ankarette Twynyho by W Wheatley (Steve Horler)

The site of this outrage is believed to be what is now 55-61 Lower Keyford though much altered.

54 The 'Nunnery' in 2018

5
EARLY MODERN 1500 – 1800

1500s Apple Alley, Frome's Oldest Street?
Tucked away between the back doors of Cheap Street and King Street lies a very narrow and little-known passageway known as Apple Alley, part of the medieval street pattern of the town with buildings surviving from the 16th century. Like many an old street the frontages are subject to alteration as they are adapted to a change of use or fashion but the backs are often left alone and ignored providing us with a better idea of a building's history.

The footpath has had a number of names in its long history including, 'Leg of Mutton Lane' in the 1840s, a reference to the shape of a block of buildings at the King Street end, 'Back Lane' in the 1880s for reasons which will be obvious but 'Apple Lane' is shown clearly on the 1774 map of the town running from the Market Place to what is now King Street.

It is roughly paved with crazy paving style sandstone slabs some with a wavy pattern indicating that they were once part of a sandy shore millions of years ago and it is possible that some of them may have come from floors of buildings demolished in around 1810 when Bath Street was cut, others match those quarried at Marston. Road surface levels tended to rise at roughly a foot per century as they were resurfaced and repaired and in Apple Alley there is a good example of this were the old

55 Apple Alley in 2018

back door of 4 Cheap Street is at least two feet below the stone paving. This particular building has a very impressive double jetty, a building technique which allowed the upper stories to project out over the ground floor thus providing more surface area without taking up more space on the ground and in use from the 14th until the 17th centuries. A very useful system in a confined space or where land was expensive. Imagine what delights could be exposed were the render to be stripped away and its timber framing revealed; of a similar age is number 11 with many internal beams and features intact and now a Grade II * listed building.

The rear of 6 Cheap Street has an original pigeon loft high up in the wall; these were used to provide meat for the table and have rarely survived in towns. They are now blocked off with netting to – keep the pigeons out - with limited success! Moving on to No.8 there is a well-preserved turret type structure containing a late 17th century winding staircase. Nos 9,10 & 17 were the subject of a major fire in 1923 and partly rebuilt in an industrial red brick.

The historical importance of this ancient thoroughfare was recognised in the mid 1990s and a grant of £46,000 was obtained from the Heritage Lottery Fund, Frome Town Council, Somerset County Council and Mendip for repairs to paving and lighting. The work was carried out in 1998 and the situation much improved but the pressures of modern living have not improved things with the area jammed with commercial dustbins, pigeon netting and spikes over the windows. Banks of air conditioning units disfigure the walls along with the inevitable graffiti. The attractive carved sign at the entrance now has traces of woodworm. Nonetheless to is worth a small diversion from the Market Place to get something of the feel of an ancient street.

1500s Gorehedge.
These picturesque Elizabethan cottages stood in what is now Christchurch Street East and consisted of a butcher's shop to the right and up the slope with two private dwellings in the front. The butcher Henry 'Boosey' Cray can be seen standing outside his premises and in the census of 1871, he is shown as aged 51 living there with his wife Mary and four children employing one man. He was still there in 1901, 'butcher aged 76'. The street to the right was once a continuation of Gentle Street. Despite their considerable age virtually nothing is known about them; their quaint antiquarian appearance led to them being photographed many times but their humble nature caused them to be largely ignored by the historians of the day.

Nothing was built to replace them for some time until a public convenience was constructed on the site. This served the population for many

56 Gorehedge cottages demolished c.1905

years until it was realised that the council was under no obligation to provide such services and it was in its turn demolished and replaced with a strange structure of unknown purpose.

57 Public conveniences which replaced the Elizabethan cottages until recently

1525c Early Archway Vicarage Street

This early archway lies in Vicarage Street between numbers 27 and 28. The probability is that it led to the town's ancient tithe barn and has been dated to around 1525.

58 *The Ancient Arch in Vicarage Street 1600s*

1527 St John's Burgled

John Twenowe and Thomas Tornay along with several others broken into the church through a window and stole, goods, plate and jewels which they broke out of an iron chest and 'bare away' to a goldsmith in Bristol who then sold it on to many others at way below its value. It seems that the perpetrators were 'acquitted and discharged by reason of the great bearing of divers gentlemen their friends and allies it within the shires of Wiltshire and Somerset to the ill example and comfort of all suchlike offenders'.

1540 Antiquary John Leland visits the Town

John Leland (1503-1552) was one of the earliest students of British topography, studying and recording ancient sites as well as cataloguing many libraries during the dissolution of the monasteries. He is most famous for his itineraries travelling throughout England and Wales during the summers from 1539 to 1543. He arrived at Frome in 1540:

59 John Leland

From Broke, [near Westbury] onto Frome Celwood in Somersetshire, 4 miles, much by woody ground and pasture until I came within a mile of it where there is champaine [arable]

The town hath a good market, and is set on the clefe of a stony hill.

There is a goodly large Paroche Church in it, and a right fair spring in the churchyard that by pipes and trenches is conveyed to divers parts of the town. There be divers fair stone houses in the town that stand the most by clothing.

In the bottom of the town runneth Frome river leaving the town on the left, and there is a Stone bridge of five arches. Then about 2 miles I came to a bottom where another brook ran into Frome and in this bottom dwell certain good clothiers having fair houses and tucking Mills.

[This was on the road from Frome to Norton St Philip -either Spring Gardens or Shawford]

1568 The Waggon and Horses, Gentle Street.
Gentle Street, the cobbled thoroughfare which even today retains much of its old world charm, is the location for one of Frome's oldest taverns. First mentioned in 1568, some of its 16th century interior is still visible today. In its heyday this was one of Frome's main coaching inns and derived its name from the wagons or coaches leaving en route for London. This side to the business continued for upwards of a century.

It was from Joseph Clavey's yard known as Clavey's Barton behind the inn that the stagecoach, the Frome Flyer, would depart for London each Monday at 1pm during the early 1700s, reaching Holborn by noon two days later. The return coach left at 1pm each Thursday and reached Frome at noon on Saturdays, stopping at Amesbury, Heytesbury and Warminster. The horses had to be changed at least every twenty miles and for a fare of eight shillings a traveller could bring 14lbs of luggage with them on this arduous journey. The

60 The Waggon and Horses in about 1900

coaching yard is now a small, private car-park.

In November 1761 it was reported that,

> a Stag was turned out in Long-Leat Park by Lord Weymouth and some other gentlemen, which shewed fine sport for some Miles; when taking into the Turnpike road he ran into Frome, and making into a Public-House, the Sign of the Waggon and Horses, took Shelter in the cellar, where he was pursued, and taken alive under a Butt of stale Beer.

Why would Lord Weymouth have been permitted to extend his hunt onto the premises of the Waggon and Horses? Well, because he owned it – the inn was part of the extensive Longleat Estate and remained so until 1919 when it was auctioned off. All licensees on the estate were Longleat tenants.

From at least the early 1770s David French was the licensed victualler at the Waggon and Horses and at this time Gentle Street was still known to many by its far less relaxing soubriquet of Hunger Lane and David and Hester French owned a number of properties there. In August 1782 tragedy struck when their only son was accidentally shot dead by a friend when they were out shooting for the day. By the time Hester died in April 1784 their daughter

Sarah had, like so many publican's daughters, married another inn holder in Frome, Charles Romaine. They were running their own inn so when David French died or retired there was no family left to take over and the inn passed from the French family.

A newspaper report of 1846 gives the pub a bad reputation and contains the damning words, 'the dissipated of both sexes are in the habit of repairing to this inn'.

61 Revealing the ancient fireplace in the old taproom to show the many forms in which it has been used over the centuries. To the left (top) a hole in the wall leads through to a disused stairwell.

Evidently the bad reputation continued despite the noble attempts of various landlords. During the early 1860s William Pitman was proprietor. He was licensed to sell both wines and spirits, maintained a fine bowling alley and held an 'ordinary' (social dance) each Wednesday. Pitman was also a member of the Frome Volunteers, which evidently did little to earn him respect for in November 1866 John Holloway, 'a young man of respectable parentage', was gaoled for two months hard labour for stealing a basket containing vegetables from the Waggon and Horses.

Permitting prostitutes to gather in a public house, sometimes euphemistically referred to a keeping a 'disorderly house', was the cause of many landlords' falling foul of the law in the mid 1800s. In February 1868 Charles Knapton was fined for having 'knowingly permitted divers persons of notoriously bad character to assemble in his house'. PC William Lock had found four prostitutes there drinking with five completely inebriated customers. The only defence Knapton could offer was that he had not been at the house long and had not acquainted himself with the local characters. It was not really a good enough explanation and the bench fined him £2, describing it as an 'abominable case' and threatening to impose a £10 if he appeared before them again.

Historically inns were often used to hold inquests. An altogether convenient arrangement, especially if the deceased was a member of the publican's own family as happened in 1883 when 55-year-old Mary Summerhayes, wife of the landlord, was found dead in her bed. She had a heart complaint it seems, and it was deemed to be natural causes.

The following year the new landlord James Maundrell found a small boy asleep in a wagon in the yard at the back. He took the child, twelve year old Herbert Henry Bendle, to the police station where the reasons for his open air sojourn were uncovered. He had truanted from school, and not for the first time. Young Henry was brought up before the magistrates on a charge of vagrancy. The magistrates dismissed the case with a warning that if the boy re-offended he would be sent to the industrial school. In 1919 the Waggon and

62 *Waggon & Horses in 1949*

Horses, now leased to Frome United Brewery, was finally sold by the Longleat Estate, described in the sale particulars as:

> Bar, Bar Parlour, Servery, Two Sitting Rooms, Kitchen, Wash-house and Cellar, with 5 bedrooms, and 2 Attics over .... In the Yard adjoining, which is approached from Blind House lane, is a commodious Range of Outbuildings [including] Cart Shed ... Large Wagon Shed .... 4-stall Stable ... 6-stall Stable ... Poultry House ..., old Skittle Alley (now converted into Pig sty) ... Large Clubroom and Ante-room approached by separate staircase.

The old place finally closed as a public house in 1959 and by 1963 had fallen into disrepair with smashed windows and a sad façade of decay. It was converted into flats by Frome Urban District Council and continued to provide social housing until sold at auction in 2012. It has more recently been turned into a private family home, with many of its original features having been uncovered and restored.

1625 The Plaguy House

63 The Plague spreads from London, From Thomas Dekker's A Rod for Run-awayes *in 1625.*

Whereas it appeareth to the Courte by the petition of the Townsmen of Frome that they have disbursed the sume of eight pounds and upwards for and towards the reliefe of one Phillips his wife and child who came from London in this late time of infeccon of the plague and were shute up in a remote house from the Towne and in keeping a good gard and watche upon the said house and people.

The poor family were locked in to die having made the journey from London to seek refuge from the infection. By the end of 1625, the contagion had claimed nearly 70,000 lives across England. More than half the deaths had been in London where the disease had killed well over 35,000, in a city of fewer than 330,000 people. Many more may have been undiagnosed victims. The house itself stood on the corner of Grove Lane and Marston Road becoming a local

64 Site of the Plaguy House on the Cruse Map of 1813 plot 1414

landmark before it was demolished presumably some time before the map of 1813 which shows no building on the plot.

Dekker described that year's outbreak of plague in London, now thought to have been caused by the bacterium *Yersinia pestis* and spread by fleas on rats. Death (shown here as a skeleton, with London in the background) stands on new coffins, casting arrows at the fleeing people and saying he will follow them. The lightning overhead represents God's wrath.

1642-1660 Civil War Period.

The town survived well during the civil war, its hard-working and pragmatic attitude enabled the population to accommodate the new regime without too much trouble. Having said that, we have very little information other than reports in the churchwarden's accounts which tell how in 1643 a troop of Royalist soldiers were billeted in the church on their way to Bradford on Avon, the churchwardens having to pay two shillings to clean up after them. It is claimed that the church bells were rung to celebrate Parliamentary victory but never a Royalist one There are no reports of fighting in the town.

> Paid to Mr Avery for writing of a certificate to send to the Parliament to certify them that the painted glass in the church windows was taken down.

> Paid to Thomas Clements for ropes for the bells which were used before the wars began.

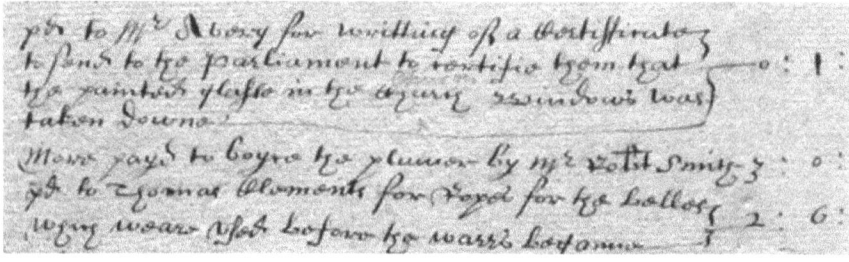

65 *Two entries in the churchwardens account to book for 1643*

The King's Arms managed to survive in the church until 1651 when Will Crease was paid 2/-for lime for 'defasing and white lyming the late Kings Arms.' In the same year was 'paid the ringers after the Worcester fight 2/6,' this in celebration of the defeat of the Royalist troops on 3 December. In 1658 beer was given to drummer Richard Wayland for the proclaiming of Richard, son of Oliver Cromwell, as Lord Protector and 5/- was given for wood for a bonfire at the same time.

Keeping up with the times, in 1660 following the restoration, the king's arms were replaced by a John Richard who was paid 1/4/- for 'cleaning up the place to set up the king's arms and paid a painter for setting up the arms 2/-. One notable event of the time was the siege of Nunney Castle about four miles distant. The castle was in the possession of the Prater family, Richard Prater being a colonel in the Royalist army. In September 1644 it was besieged by General Fairfax having failed to surrender when ordered. In military terms

66 Nunney Castle (Ian Alexander CC)

the castle was pretty useless being built on low ground and used more as a comfortable home. Lead was taken from the church roof of St John's in Frome to make bullets for the siege and the castle soon fell after which it was gutted by order of Cromwell's Parliament creating the ruin we see today.

1660 The Black Boy, Wallbridge.
There is certainly no shortage of strange names attached to the pubs of the British Isles from The Crooked Fish, The World Turned Upside Down to The Bull & Mouth. Multiple entries in the church rate books refer to various properties in Frome as 'near the Black Boy' which indicates that it must have been a prominent landmark. The name alone is of interest and there are a several possible etymologies, including references to chimney sweeps, miners and servants. The most likely origin is that it refers to King Charles II, nicknamed 'The Black Boy' by his mother Queen Henrietta on account of his swarthy appearance. Presumably his dark looks were acquired from his Italian maternal grandmother Marie de Medici and during his flight after the

disastrous Battle of Worcester wanted posters described Charles as a 'tall, black man'. In other words, the Black Boy could be seen as another name for the King's Head and there are estimated to have around 70 with that name in the country celebrating the end of the Puritan regime. It would be an interesting exercise to see if the name could be traced back to before the restoration of 1660. The name was in the news recently when in a bizarre move the brewers, Greene King decided to rename four of their pubs which contained the word black, three Black Boys and a Black's Head in case they were thought to be racist!

67 King Charles II The Black Boy

The earliest reference to the Black Boy at Frome is the payment of church rates by Henry and Walter Merchant in 1679, some eighteen years after Charles II ascended the throne. The Merchants were still there in 1693 as tenants, the pub being a part of the immense Longleat Estate holdings. In 1702 a lease was granted to Richard Rose, cordwainer, for the property 'called or known by the name of the figure of The Black Boy'. In this lease Longleat retained their rights to the timber from all trees on the property and in addition, Rose had to plant three apple or pear trees and three oak, ash or elm trees each year. John Wayland took over the lease in 1710, and in 1732 he was paying 4d. in the church rates for 'Ye Blackboy.' Wayland remained there until 1733 when a lease was granted to John Young, who died in 1748.

68 The Black Boy is shown as plot 1222/23 on the Cruse map of 1813

William Kellow, or possibly Kells, was in occupation in 1766, and seems to have been convicted for selling beer without the necessary license in 1785.

But where was it? The pub is clearly marked with its extensive orchard on a map by John Ladd of 1744 now held by the Longleat Estate and the building is shown as a 'house and garden' owned by John Meares on the Jeremiah Cruse map of 1813 plot no. 1222/3. The last known reference to the inn is in a document in Frome Museum which states, 'Black Boy taken down by John Meares' and dated 1834. The site now lies roughly beneath the B & M store and the petrol station in the area leading to Frome railway station.

1662 Joseph Glanvill, Vicar & Demonologist.

Joseph Glanvill became vicar of St John's in Frome in November 1662, two years after the restoration of the monarchy. He was born into a puritan family in Plymouth in 1636 and after Oxford he was ordained in 1660 and as with many of his kind he was far too intelligent for his profession, but the church gave him a living and the leisure time to pursue his other interests. He became disillusioned with the puritanism of his childhood which is unlikely to have gone down well with his congregation in a place of well-established protestant dissent. He was perhaps one of the most promising young academics of his age and contributed much to the revival of interest in witchcraft and other supernatural phenomena in an era of uncertainty and changing values. It has been suggested that a lot of the fear of witches and the supernatural extremely prevalent at the time was invented or at least encouraged by the church itself to frighten the population into submission. However it arose, Glanvill arrived at its height and was fascinated by it.

In the winter of 1662–3, shortly after he arrived in Frome, Glanvill visited John Mompesson at Tedworth on the edge of Salisbury Plain and spent a night at his house during which he witnessed various forms of what would now be called poltergeist activity associated with the so-called 'Drummer of Tedworth', the most famous episode of its kind at that time. Accounts report that in 1661 Mompesson had brought a lawsuit against an unlicensed vagrant drummer, William Drury, whom he accused of collecting money by false pretences. He won judgment against the drummer, whose drum was turned over to Mompesson by the local bailiff after which he found his house plagued by nocturnal drumming noises. It was alleged that the drummer had brought these plagues of noise upon Mompesson's head by witchcraft and that he was associated with a band of gypsies. During his stay Glanvill, heard strange noises under a bed in the children's room.

I heard a strange scratching as I went up the Stairs, and when we came into the Room, I perceived it was just behind the Bolster of the Children's Bed, and seemed to be against the Tick. It was as loud a scratching, as one with long Nails could make upon a Bolster. There were two little modest Girls in the Bed, between Seven and Eleven years old as I guessed. I saw their hands out over the Clothes, and they could not contribute to the noise that was behind their heads.

Despite the case being largely dismissed as historical trickery today, the cultural importance of Glanvill's work, and the ghostly drummer himself, has been significant. Even the famous diarist Samuel Pepys, wrote on Christmas day in 1667 that he had been fascinated by the story and regarded it 'worth reading indeed.'

Glanvill had already published two books, *The Vanity of Dogmatizing or Confidence in Opinions manifested in a Discourse of the Shortness and Uncertainty of our Knowledge, and it's causes with some Reflexions on Peripateticism, and an apology for Philosophy*, in 1661 and *Lux Orientalis; or an enquiry into the Opinion of the Eastern Sages concerning the Pre-Existence of Souls*, and become fascinated by the occult. He was captivated by tales of witchcraft near his home in Selwood Forest which had been recorded in a 'book of examinations' kept by local magistrate, Robert Hunt and took the various manifestations as evidence towards the existence of the soul.

In a later book *Saducismus Triumphatus*, he told the story of his experiences at Tedworth the only event of which he had personal experience and after which

Joseph Glanvill FRS (1636-80), Vicar of Frome Selwood (1662-72)

69 Joseph Glanvill

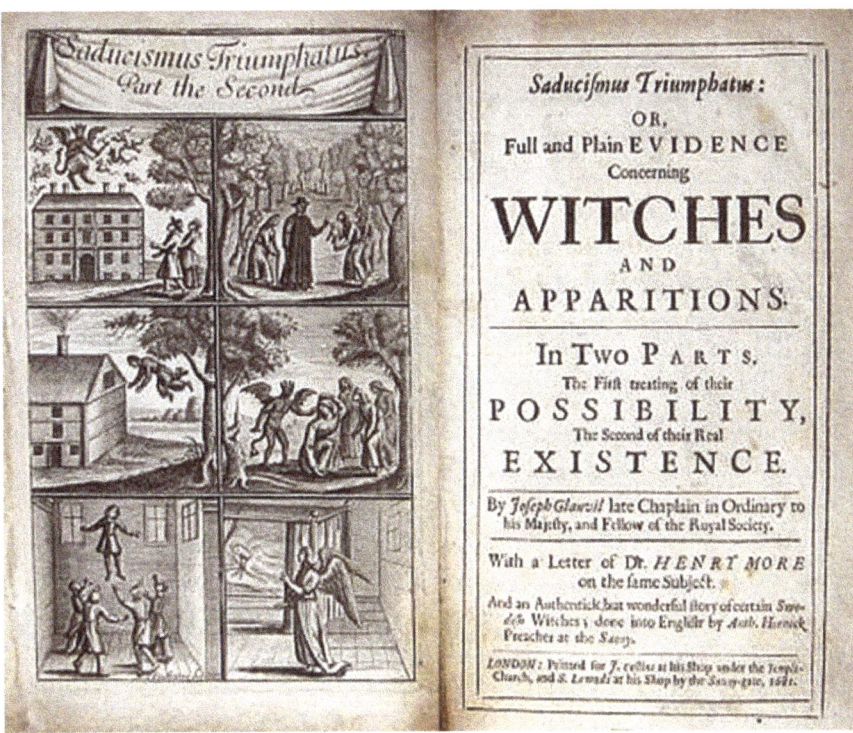

70 Glanvill's Saducismus Triumphatus

he readily accepted the validity of the accounts of respectable people as further affirmation of the reality of spirits: malign and benevolent. 'It will be said by some', he acknowledged, 'I (was) under some affright, and so fancied noises and sights that were not.' However, he contested, 'This is the eternal evasion. … I know what I heard and saw.'

In 1664 Glanvill joined the recently formed Royal Society and in the same year he began in earnest his study of poltergeists and witches. He was a most progressive thinker and fully committed to the principle of knowledge by observation and experiment over dogma. For Glanvill the suspension of disbelief when presented with evidence that defied simple explanation was 'a necessary part of the scientific attitude,' creating the paradox that Glanvill believed in witches because he was a sceptic.

In 1666 he published his findings and theories on the matter of witchcraft for the first time in *Some Philosophical Considerations Touching Witches and Witchcraft*. Throughout his writings, Glanvill adopted a scientific approach in advancing empirical evidence and historical precedent as proof for the existence of spirits and witchcraft rather than relying exclusively on theology and biblical texts. 'All histories', he declared, 'are full of the exploits of those instruments of darkness, and the testimony of all ages, not only of the rude and barbarous, but of the most civilised and polished world, brings tidings of their strange performances.' These provided 'thousands of eye and ear-witnesses' drawn from all social groups including many 'wise and grave discerners.' To deny them amounted to the absurd possibility that they were all engaged in a monstrous lie and to reject this mountain of evidence required, in Glanvill's opinion, a vastly bigger leap of faith than to accept it as fact.

Science, Glanvill maintained, was not the enemy of religion but the antidote to atheism. Science might yet prove certain key religious doctrines, notably that of belief in the supernatural. In Glanvill's opinion the evidence was overwhelming and 'Matters of fact well proved ought not to be denied because we cannot conceive how they can be performed.' 'On the contrary, we should judge the action by the evidence, and not by the measures of our fancies about the action.'

Glanvill was widely regarded as the great authority on the supernatural and without his study of the many cases in and around the Frome area it seems unlikely that our knowledge of certain cases would be as comprehensive as it is. Glanvill did not live to see the *Saducismus* printed, dying of fever on 4 November 1680 at the age of forty-five, He was buried in Bath Abbey where his commemorative stone in the floor, partly obscured by pews, can still be seen.

1667 Frome Bridge Rebuilt.

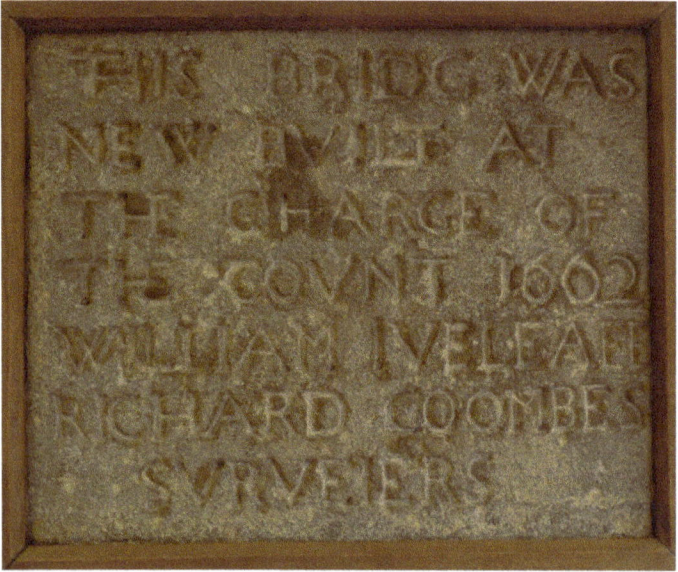

71 The plaque at 4 The Bridge

A plaque now built into an inside wall at 4 The Bridge reads, 'This bridge was new built at the charge of the county 1667 William Iveleafe Richard Coombs surveiers'.

1668 The Fair Maids of Foxcote
The church of SS Phillip and James dates in part from the 13th century and contains the grave, or at least a memorial to 'The Fair Maids of Foscott'. The Maids were Siamese twins first mentioned by diarist Samuel Pepys in June of 1668 when he visited the church and saw their tomb.

72 The Fair Maids

> At Philips Norton I walked to the church, and there saw a very ancient tomb of some Knight Templar, I think; and here saw the tombstone whereon there were only two heads cut, which, the story goes, and credibly, were two sisters called the Fair Maids of Foscott, that had two bodies upward and one belly and there lie buried. Here is also a very fine ring of six bells, and they mighty tuneable. (www.pepysdiary.com/diary/1668/06/12/)

Tradition has it that they lived to reach a 'state of maturity and that one of them dying the survivor was constrained to drag about her lifeless companion until death released her of her horrid burden'. Given the twins must have been one of the wonders of the age it is strange that so little is known about them, including their names and even the century in which they lived. When Pepys saw the tomb, the effigy of the two sisters was cut in stone on the floor of the nave. This was removed probably as part of a restoration in the 1840s, except for the two heads which were saved and fixed to the wall inside the tower. Foscott is a hamlet, a few miles from Norton, now named Foxcote.

1685 The Monmouth Rebellion.
James Scott, Duke of Monmouth, was the illegitimate son of Charles II, and as such claimed to be the rightful heir to the throne. After the death of Charles in 1685, Monmouth landed at Lyme Regis with the intention of overthrowing his uncle, James II formally the Duke of York but now the newly crowned king. He marched north into Somerset to rouse support and at its peak it was said his 'army' consisted of around 7,000 rebels. However, by the time the rain-sodden duke and his men arrived in Frome, on 28 June 1685 the tide had begun to turn.

A letter from Thomas Allen a steward at Longleat to his master Viscount Weymouth describes the events,

> I believe your lordship hath more certain intelligence of what past in the action on Saturday at Phillips Norton than we have. The Duke's party gave out that they killed 80 and lost but 5 and none of the kings side do you come this way to contradict it. They entered Frome yesterday at four in the morning very wet and weary. I believe they will march this day to Warminster and call here as they go. Capt. Kid sent yesterday to T.Pierce desiring him to come to him. I went along with him, and found the town full of armed men and horses, but cannot judge what number unless I could see them drawn out into the field.

The report themselves to be 30,000, but if they be so many, the greatest part were asleep whilst I was there. The Duke rode around the town once in two hours, they call him King there as confidently as if he had the crown on his head, and when they speak of his Majesty they call him York.

Whilst I was at the Bell there came some to put up their horses, Chapman the landlord denied then saying he had four score of the Kings horses already. And when the people ran to see him,

(Monmouth) they asked if the king were gone by.

from the Thynne Papers, Longleat XXII folio 185R

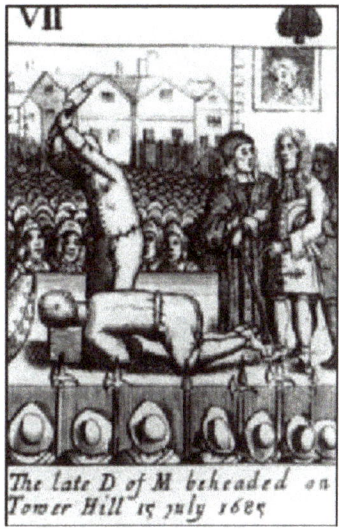
73 A playing card depicting the end of James, Duke of Monmouth

On 25 June while Monmouth was in retreat from Bristol, Robert Smith the constable of Frome posted a declaration in the town declaring Monmouth

74 Monmouth Chambers Cork Street. The building survives despite some determined attempts to demolish it in 1970.

the rightful king. This was soon torn down and the main instigators arrested. While in staying in Cork Street, Monmouth learnt that a simultaneous rebellion in Scotland had been defeated and royal forces were massing in Trowbridge. Worse was to come. The following day, James II issued a pardon for all who had taken up arms, and many rebels took the opportunity to return home. A war council was hastily called and against Monmouth's belief that he should now return into exile, he was forcibly told by his generals he must fight on. Monmouth and what, were left of his rapidly dispersing army left Frome on 30 June 1685 and headed west towards his destiny at the Battle of Sedgemoor. Within a little over a fortnight of leaving Frome he would be dead; having been defeated, found guilty of treason and then executed on London's Tower Hill. After Monmouth left the town, royal troops entered and 'plundered' it, although this was only the start of the retribution. At the subsequent trials - known as the Bloody Assizes - fifty Frome men were tried and found guilty of treason; being either executed or like constable Smith, transported for life. While back in Frome, 12 rebels found guilty at the Assizes were hung, drawn and quartered and their remains strung up at Gibbet Hill.

75 The Frome Society Plaque

1691 The Blue Boar, 15 Market Place.
The Blue Boar in the Market Place has the distinction of being one of the oldest of Frome's 14 or so surviving pubs and was built by a Theophilus Lacey who took on a lease for 99 years from 3 November 1691.

In the 1720s a lock-up was built abutting the pub and years later Frome town constable Isaac Gregory was there to keep an eye on things. In March 1818 he was in no mood for petty squabbles, 'Sent for in haste to the Blue Boar 2 men was fighting in the parlour one of the men lost his hat and had his cloths much torn, it served him right as he had no business there and he had no pity from me'.

There was more violence afoot in 1823 when a man was killed just outside after a quarrel over some beer John Crees died after the fight which resulted in convictions for manslaughter. A little later the pub was used as an annex to the lock-up when George Howarth, part of a notorious criminal gang was caught stealing wood from a timber yard nearby. After a ferocious fight he was wounded, arrested, and taken to the pub to have his wounds dressed. During the night Howarth escaped by leaping out of a window 20 feet high into the water and gaining the opposite bank. He was free for several weeks before being recaptured and transported for life.

Despite the obvious folly of using a pub bedroom for a prison, in August of 1844 a Mr. Batt tried to sell a stolen horse. He was imprisoned in the very same room from which George Howarth had escaped nearly 20 years before. On Sunday night the padlock was secured and 'all was right' but come Monday morning, 'an open casement and yards of bed cord hanging outside the window, told the fact of how the constables were regularly done.'

In January of 1857, when Superintendent Summers heard a great noise coming from the pub after hours he organised a raid and claimed to have found 40 or 50 people inside many of them drunk and some who couldn't stand up – not a sober man there. Also on the scene was the Parish Constable, Mr. Newport who was asked make a note of those present, 'I went home to get my pencil to take down the names of the people in the room. There was no noise or improper conduct that I saw nor was there anyone drunk.' Newport's evidence directly contradicted that of the police as did the evidence of those

76 The Blue Boar of 1691

present - not surprisingly. To make things worse some of the defence witnesses claimed that there had been a band playing and others that there had been no band at all. Despite all concerned making a complete dog's dinner of the case the bench assumed that something had been going on and, 'The evidence for the defence being contradictory, defendant was fined 40/- and 6/10d costs.'

In 1861 the Boar was the scene of what was one of the town's most incompetent attempts at theft. James Ruddock having 'possessed himself of the pub curtain unperceived' nips over the road to the Black Swan and tries to sell it. Having no luck he takes it back to the Blue Boar and – gets arrested!

Silas Goddard a tailor 'whose garments were out of repair and who was the possessor of a wooden leg' was in trouble in 1868 when he was found to be swearing and wanting to fight someone, eventually pushing Mr. Harvey, the landlord, down. PC Watts went to assist 'when he received a poke in the side from the prisoner's wooden leg. Prisoner flourished his timber member violently and boasted of its various uses and the advantages derived from it compared with its predecessor. Some broken heads would have been the result had not PC Watts unscrewed the leg and took it away'. Fined £20 or two months hard labour.

1696 Iron Gates, King Street

77 Iron Gates in 2019

Built by the Sheppard family, major clothiers in the town, but much altered in the mid 18th century Iron Gates survives as a fine Georgian house now used as commercial premises. The Sheppards continued to occupy it until 1895 and it is now a Grade 1 listed building of national importance which did not prevent its distinctive garden from being destroyed and incorporated into the dreadful 1970s Kingsway shopping precinct. Adjoining it from the rear is what is known as the Courthouse although there is no record of it having been used as such. It has a fine shell hood over the entrance and at the time of writing is undergoing restoration.

78 The Court House under Restoration

1720s Lock-ups & Blind Houses.

The Frome Guardhouse
Until the building of the Frome police station in 1857, anyone found breaking the law, being drunk and disorderly or generally making of a nuisance of themselves ended up in what was known as the guardhouse next to the Blue Boar pub in the Market Place. It was built by 1728 but we know from Abraham Crocker's plan of 1808 that the building was extended at a later date as this map shows a much smaller building than that shown in more recent photos.

The map reference book states that plot 10a was owned by the Earl of Cork and occupied as 'Guard house of Court' and occupied by Peace Officers.

The spot chosen was convenient for the nearby magistrate's court, which was at the end of Edgell's Lane, now Justice Lane and is part of the Cheese & Grain car park opposite the round tower. In various accounts of the town the terms 'blind house' (ie no windows), 'lock up' and 'guard house' are used interchangeably.

When Isaac Gregory was constable of Frome during the 1800s, he kept

79 Crocker's Map of 1808: Guardhouse 10a, Blue House 7a, Blue Boar 11

80 The Guardhouse shortly before its demolition in 1965

journals which have numerous references to the guardhouse and the various miscreants he had occasion to lock up there. These included 'two little boys', confined for 'a few minutes' in 1813 for stealing seven shillings from their parents, while the next year an older boy received an hour's confinement for 'being impudent to me'. It was not only children who caused Gregory trouble though. One man spent a night behind bars after becoming abusive when denied beer after 10 o'clock at night in the Eagle Inn (at the end of Eagle Lane).

Many a Frome drunk slept it off in the guardhouse and one was John Crees who in 1823, after getting into a drunken argument in the Blue Boar, was savagely attacked outside in the Market Place. A constable, not realising how serious the man's injuries were, took him to the guardhouse by to sleep it off. Unfortunately, as he did not receive the medical treatment required, he died soon afterwards. Those fortunate to make it through the night were let out the next morning and taken across the road or, if their crime was more serious, escorted to Shepton Mallet jail, fifteen miles away.

Among the more hardened criminals who experienced the latter were the trio of suspects in the infamous killing of 14-year-old Sarah Watts, in 1851, who was brutally murdered on a West Woodlands farm. The 'Frome Three', consisted of William Sparrow, William Maggs and Robert Hurd, aka 'Frome Bob'.

The Blue House was renovated once more in 1965 which also resulted in the destruction of the guard house which had been used as storage for the market stalls and a public lavatory. The left hand wall survives as a tall pillar at the end of the Blue Boar pub.

The Blindhouse of 1798

The Blindhouse was, and incredibly, still is, situated in the south-east corner of St John's churchyard it has a date stone of 1798 and was built as a replacement for another on the corner of Church Street and Vicarage Street which obstructed what traffic there was in those days and moved to its present location with the Bishop of Bristol arriving to reconsecrate the churchyard.

It consists of an underground stone-vaulted cell with a stone slated roof, but no windows, although a small opening allowed relatives to lower food in. This was cleaned up and restored by the Frome Civic Society in 1980 but is now again much dilapidated. Its blocked-up doorways can still be seen in Blindhouse Lane.

81 The Blocked Doorway in Blindhouse Lane (above).

1720 The Blue House.

82 The Blindhouse entrance in 2023 (right)

One of Frome's most famous and iconic buildings is an ancient almshouse known as the Blue House which stands beside the bridge as the Market Place is entered from the north. The building we see today was completed in 1728 and paid for by a public subscription launched by local solicitor James

83 Philip Crocker's drawing of 1802. Town Bridge with Blue House to the left

Wickham which raised the huge total of £1,087, the build costing £1401/8/9 in total. The new building is probably the third on the site and besides the main building, the price covered the re-construction of two arches of the town bridge, a guardhouse and various walls. Also included were payments of £12. 8s. for the well-known figures of Nancy Guy and Billy Ball and £22 for the clock made by James Clark. The building swallowed 48,000 laths and 12,240 feet of oak board.

A house for the poor had stood on the same site for more than 500 years when William Leversedge, Lord of the Manor decided to do something about the poor and infirm people of the town. William's almshouse consisted of a hall, chapel and twelve chambers and was endowed with four and a half acres of land. Little is recorded of its early history but by the 16th century it was receiving benefactions from Frome people. As early as 1538 William Kyppinge, of Buckland, left six cows for the relief of the 'poure people' in the almshouse on condition that the profits were spent 'in mete and drynke and not in reparations', a bequest that suggests the buildings already needed repair. Again, in 1543, William Catcote left 4d. each 'to every poor person of the Almshouse in Frome'. The revenues from the four acre endowment were earmarked for the maintenance of 'twelve poor people, men and women, born or to be born in the said Parish of Froome to dwell and be resident' there. No men seem to have been provided for in the early days, probably because the charity was not rich enough to provide separate accommodation for them.

The Almshouse already occupied its present site in 1652 when it is described as 'scituate neere the greate Bridge in the Towne of Froome Sellwood'. There are no records of gifts of land up to this date on which it might have been rebuilt so it has probably always been where it stands today. In 1644, 'all that messuage or house called the

84 The Blue House today (Andrea Brooke)

Almeshouse' with gardens to the north and south was conveyed to new trustees together with land in the North Field of Frome, in Nunney and at Garston stile.

The doorcase on the present building has a fashionable pediment and bolection moulding. A hipped roof with cupola and clock crowns the whole imposing edifice. It would not be out of place in Bath, Bristol or any other Georgian city and has been described as 'an admirable work of vernacular baroque'. The central part was intended for the school and in contrast are the plain recessed wings with their old-fashioned mullioned windows, and chimneys set centrally in their facades, which were reserved for the almswomen. The building became known as the Blue House, or the Blue School from the knee-length blue coats with brass buttons worn by the schoolboys.

During the 19th century the Blue House fell on bad days. In 1866, it was 'much in want of repair', and restored by the trustees. According to *Kelly's Directory of Somerset*, there were 25 residents in 1894 'each of whom has a weekly allowance of 5s or 5s.6d. and a furnished room; there are also two nurses who receive a weekly salary'. The endowments were then valued at £8,802 which produced £446. 12s. a year. Although the building remained broadly sound, it needed a thorough overhaul. Those who knew it after the Second World War remember it as grim and bleak. It was four storeys high, subject to flooding and inadequately heated, hardly up to modern standards for the care of the elderly.

In the early 1960s the threat of demolition loomed large once more with the prospect of the residents being whisked away from what had become their home. Money was raised and a major overhaul undertaken resulting in comfortable flats at reasonable rents for the town's aged residents.

1724 Daniel Defoe visits Froom.
Defoe, author of *Gulliver's Travels* was impressed with the town and made two entries in his journal, *A Tour Thro the Whole of the Island of Great Britain* noting that had recently been constructed,

a new church and so many new streets of houses that those houses are so full of inhabitants that Frome is now reckoned to have more people in it than the city of

85 Daniel Defoe

Bath, and some say then even of Salisbury itself, and if their trade continues to increase for a few more years as it has done in the past it is very likely to be one of the greatest and wealthiest inland towns in England.

Its trade is wholly clothing and the cloths they make are, generally speaking all conveyed to London: Blackwell Hall is their market and if we believe common fame, there are above 10,000 people in Frome now, more than lived in at 20 years ago and get it was a considerable town then too.

1726 The Weavers Riot.
The weavers rioted in November of this year due to sharp practice on behalf of the clothiers who had introduced a 17lb weight for weighing the cloth that was brought to them for sale and lengthening the warping bars on the looms so that the weavers had to weave a broader cloth for the same pay. The government was disturbed at the extent of the disturbance and sent in the dragoons whose commander, Colonel Paulet described the weavers as,

The most notorious rioters' claiming that his troops had been much insulted,

86 Blackwell Hall in the City of London was the centre for the wool and cloth trade from medieval times until 1812. Cloth manufacturers and clothiers from provincial England brought their material here to display and sell to merchants and drapers. Shown being demolished in 1812.

and that 'Frome was a Jacobite place' and he believed the clothiers houses would be destroyed if his troops were withdrawn. He had received an order from the magistrates to, 'fire ball if more than 20 should come to the town in a riotous matter.

A meeting of the contending parties was called and the matter seems to have been resolved - for now.

The early 1740s brought problems of a different kind with reports of a steep decline in trade due to war disrupting export to the continent.

1746 From Simpson's, 'The Agreeable Historian'.

Frome contains near as many houses as Bath and Wells put together, and four times the number of people at Wells does although it is larger than some cities… the inhabitants are reckoned to be about 13,000 of whom 'tis said one half are newcomers within these 35 years; in which time they have not been less than 2,000 houses built on new foundations. They are not indeed very sumptuous, nor the streets very spacious, the latter especially being irregular and for the greatest part up hill and down hill. 'Twas governed formerly by a Bailiff and now by two constables of the Hundred of Frome, chosen at the court Leet. The inhabitants of this town who had shown their zeal for the Glorious Revolution, endeavoured in the reign of King William to procure a charter of incorporation but in vain because they were opposed in it by a neighbouring Lord.

The woollen manufacture has thrived here to such a degree that seven wagons have been set out with cloth weekly from this town for Blackwell Hall etc. Indeed, all of it was not made in Frome for the clothiers of the neighbouring village of Elm, Mells, Whatley, Nunney, etc brought their goods hither for carriage to London and each of these wagons used to hold 140 pieces, which being valued at £14 one with another made the value of the whole amount in the year to above £700,000 in this quarter of the county. Thirty years ago more wire cards for carding the wool for the spinners were made here than in all England besides Leeds, Halifax, and other times in Yorkshire… there were no less then 20 Master Cardmakers one of whom employed 400 men women and children in making them, for even children of seven or eight years of age could earn half a crown a week.

This shows how much the concern and dependence of this town have been upon the woollen manufacture which though it has declined much here for the 10 years past still employs a great number of hands and by late advices from these parts it is reviving. The cloths made here are the most part medleys of about seven or eight shillings a yard.

The river here which abounds with trout, eels etc rises in the Woodlands and runs under a stone bridge towards Bath on the east side and falls into the Avon. This town has been a long time particularly noted for its rare, fine beer which they keep to a great age, and it is not only the nectar of the common people, but is often preferred by the gentry to the wines of France and Portugal.

1757 Food Riots.
Serious unrest occurred in the town in this year due to the high price of food. The ever troublesome colliers from Coleford and mines around Radstock were at the heart of it. In April 200 of them broke into a mealman's house (a dealer in grain), and had to be suppressed by a party of soldiers from Bruton. The following May a mob of women upset the market in trying to get the potatoes reduced by half and at the end of the month a correspondent from the *London Chronicle* reported,

> I had a very disagreeable sight of the two men that were killed and four wounded in a riot of the colliers that morning, (27 May), aside off Frome where in a quarter of an hours time they entirely pulled down and destroyed a flour mill , [belonging to a Mr Naish at Murtry] and were marching to do the same to another at a little distance, [Mr Richard's Mill] but met with so warm a reception from eight persons only, well armed with a blunderbuss, guns and pistols that their whole body, amounting to 400-500 were entirely routed, leaving two dead and wounded abovementioned behind them, three of whom

87 A riot over the price of food

are also since died of their wounds. One man had 16 balls or slugs through the brim of his hat and received no hurt. The valiant miller of the second mill had a blunderbuss which he told me with some pleasure would carry 18 balls complete at one charge'.

Mr Richards, it seems, had been attacked some six weeks earlier and was expecting another visit and so stockpiled the arms.

1757 The Turnpike Act.
From the late 17th century, Parliament increased its responsibility for repairing and maintaining roads from local authorities. Turnpike Acts authorised a trust to levy tolls on those using the road and to use that income to repair and improve them. This helped to improve the main roads between Warminster, Bath, Limpley Stoke and Shepton Mallet, a ring of tollhouses encircling the town, at the bottom of Styles Hill on the Warminster Road, Bulls Bridge junction on the Maiden Bradley Road, at the junction of Marston Road with Marston Back Lane on the Shepton Mallet Road, at Cottles Oak on the road to Mells and Whatley, at Murtry cross roads on the Radstock Road and in Spring Road on the route to Bath. Some of these and others further along the roads are still in existence.

This gradual improvement meant that the cloth and coal industries could transport their products more easily by cart without having to rely on packhorses.

88 Goose Marsh Toll Gate (1813 Cruse Atlas)

1763 Daniel Neale, Frome's Highwayman.
The 18th century was undoubtedly the golden age for the highwayman and romantic stories of the gentleman thief on horseback holding up stage coaches abound, what is not so well-known is that Frome once had its very own highwayman. The little we know begins with a report in the *Gloucester Journal* for Monday 4 July 1763:-

We have received the following particulars of a most audacious villain that has this week infested the roads between this place and Bath. On Wednesday morning he attacked, near the monument at Lansdown, two persons whom he robbed of some small sums, and afterwards coming to the turnpike on this side of the down, he found there a man who was paying for passing through, on which the highwayman ordered the turnpike man to go into his house and shut the door, or he would blow his brains out, saying, *I'll receive this gentleman's money*, and accordingly robbed the person of a considerable sum. He then came on to a little ale-house on the cross road, where he put up his horse and staid half an hour, and having drunk a quart of strong beer, and fed his horse, and set off for Tetbury.

Upon the road near Petty France he robbed a gentleman's servant of eight guineas, and soon after, meeting with a man returning from Tetbury market, near Dunkirk, he demanded his money. The man, who had a little boy before him, told the villain that he had none. He then demanded his watch, and endeavoured to pull it out of his pocket by the string, which in the struggle broke, and the man refusing to give it him, he said, *Do you contest with me?*, and lodged three slugs in the poor man's breast, of which he died soon after. He was described as a short young man, about 18, pitted much with the small pox, well-mounted on a dark brown mare, which is blind of one eye, and has a switch tail. One of his stirrups is new, the other is an old one.

It was almost a month later that perpetrator was caught as another item

89 The former Black Swan in Bridge Street

from the *Gloucester Journal* for Monday 25 July 1763 reports :-

> Another victim, drawn to the commotion, immediately declared that he was the fellow who had robbed him in the morning. *And will you swear to that?* said the highwayman. To which the other replied in the affirmative. *Why then* says the villain, *I may as well die first as last*, and with the knife with which he was eating his supper cut his throat in a shocking manner. He was not dead yesterday morning, but it was thought he could not live till night.

It emerged that Frome's 'gentleman of the road' was actually from Gloucestershire but living in Frome where he 'worked at the clothing business'. He was Daniel Neale whose wife ran a clothing shop in the town. He is known to have borrowed a mare from the landlord of the Black Swan in Bridge Street at various times on the pretence of 'going on journeys for gentlemen' presumably part of his cover story was that he was travelling with samples of cloth, and was away for up to a fortnight at a time.

Neale recovered from his injuries and stood trial at the Gloucester Assizes charged with three other robberies, *The Gloucester Journal* 22 August 1763 reports:-

> Neale, the highwayman, relates that he launched forth into this scene of villainy a few weeks before Easter last, with two accomplices, whose names he will not discover, but acknowledges that they live near Frome. He says it was to supply themselves with cash for the cockpit and the ale-house that they took to the highway, and that they have committed many robberies. Cutting cloth from clothiers racks was another part of their employ, as the inhabitants of Shepton Mallet have experienced to their cost. He confesses that they had formed a grand scheme of robbery to be carried into execution as soon as good horses and pistols could be procured, and to elude circumstantial descriptions of their persons, they had concluded in the following stratagem, to meet every night at a certain rendezvous, and there change each other's cloths, horses etc. The conviction of this enterprising villain is, therefore a most fortunate event for this and the neighbouring counties. The execution is fixed for Friday.

Apart from his short stature and pock marked face the one-eyed mare with a false tail is what the victims remembered most about their assailant .

Neale was hanged at the village of Over two miles west of Gloucester on Friday 26 August and it was reported that, 'Neale expressed great terror at the approach of death and seemed to think that his sins had been too great to be expiated by so short a repentance; and prolonged the moment in which he was to be turned off to the very last.'

Why someone so young and established in business with a wife and daughter should embark on such a drastic course we can only guess at. Drink? Gambling? Or just youthful bravado? We will never know.

1767 Thomas Bunn:- A Frome Visionary Born
Our town has had its share of philanthropists and eccentrics but perhaps the finest of them was Thomas Bunn who lived from 1767 to 1853. The son of a doctor whose portrait hangs in Frome Museum he was a solicitor by trade but hardly ever felt the need to practice having been left a large amount of money. He devoted his time and energy to helping others and being of what he described as a 'reflective disposition' he kept a diary from 1836 until 1850.

Bunn lived in Monmouth House in what is now Cork Street just off the Market Place and was responsible for the building of the old Market House adjoining the George Hotel, formerly the NatWest Bank in about 1818. The building required that he give up part of his garden which he did willingly. Bunn was an enthusiastic fan of classical architecture and wanted to see his home town resemble the wonders of Bath. His mind teamed with ideas for improvements to the town many to be financed by himself, he was obsessed with widening roads and creating sweeping thoroughfares which if achieved would have spoilt much of Frome's old-fashioned charm. Despite being a solicitor, his will, which ran to 85 pages, was so confused in its enthusiasm to devote his fortune to promote multiple projects in the town that it was discarded and all his money went to his relatives.

Still standing in Christchurch Street West and Wesley Close are two hefty stone pillars which he had erected in 1846 and which were intended to mark the beginning of one his grand avenues – standing 400 feet apart and to be modelled on Union Street in Bath. Perhaps his greatest and most lasting achievement was the cutting of Bath

90 One of the two Bunn columns set to mark his grand crescent

Street which still runs from the Market Place to Christchurch Street and is the main road out of town to the south. This was first mapped in around 1808 and some of the original sketches are still in Frome Museum. It was he who planted the magnificent Cedar of Lebanon tree along its route in the garden of no 14 in 1815. There were originally two cedar trees along with many shrubs and trees that he planted along the way and paid for himself, but the other one died in the early part of the 20th century.

As well as his architectural ambitions he was on the committee of many of the Frome charities and a leading light in the establishment of the Frome Literary Institution which eventually ended its days in the building that is now the town museum at the end of North Parade. Amongst many other good causes Bunn was a contributor and subscriber to the British and Foreign Anti-Slavery Society. Legend has it that he would let coins slip from his pockets as he walked down the street not wanting to see who picked them up and saving their embarrassment. He was married for only two years before his wife died after which he lived with his sister at Monmouth House and died at the age of 86 in May 1853.

The Frome Society is responsible for the upkeep of Bunn's grave which is in the churchyard at Christchurch marked by a large conifer tree.

Many extracts from Bunn's diaries are contained in a book by Derek Gill, published by the Frome Society and entitled *Experiences of a 19c Gentleman*. The work is divided into a number of sections like Education, Property, Health and Street Development and provides a unique view of the town in early Victorian times.

1770 Fleur De Luce Inn. Corner of Stony Street & Palmer Street.

Few people realise as they down a glass of Merlot and munch their way through a freshly made pizza at the Stony Street House wine bar that they are dining on the site of one of Frome ancient lost hostelries. Its origins are unknown but in 1749 Lionel Seaman owner of a good deal of land in Frome sold, 'all that messuage or tenement and inn called Flower de Luce Inn with all the outbuildings' to Lord Cork. This is the oldest known reference to the pub from a deed in the Somerset Record Office The lease was put up for auction again in 1763 and it was probably then that a James Hiscox became the licensee.

During this period the army sent parties of soldiers to various towns on recruitment drives and were entitled to demand seven days bed & board at a local inn while searching the area for suitable men. The billeting was arranged by the local constable who had the power to insist that the innkeeper provide for their needs at a rate of 4d per day. Part of their task was to spend a day or two at nearby fairs and markets looking for men who wanted to enlist. Their reading of the act was that they were then entitled to return to the town and receive another seven days free board at a different inn thus making the innkeepers 'perpetually burdened.' The notebooks of Thomas Horner, a local magistrate for May and June 1770 record that 'James Hiscox, innholder was summonsed for refusing to receive two soldiers employed in recruiting, and to furnish them with victuals for seven days.'

91 The Fleur up for sale, 1763

Hiscox felt that he had a good case as the complainants acknowledged that they had been at other alehouses for seven days or more, his point was that this was unfair as there were a number of recruiting parties in the town and on that interpretation of the act the constable might as well be expected to move the parties around continually from pub to pub for seven days at a time whether they left town or not and that it was an attempt to avoid the terms of the Act of Parliament. James Hiscox also ran or owned The Talbot in Trooper Street so maybe he was liable to suffer more than most which is why he refused to take them in and ended up in court. Presumably the bench accepted his case as the matter is not mentioned again.

In November 1773 another landlord Henry Box claimed that Abraham Saunders entered his pub at the head of a mob assaulted him and tore his 'cloths'. He also alleged that Saunders was 'wandering about the country exhibiting for gain, puppet shows, juggling etc' contrary to the Vagrancy Act. It seems that the case was contrived by Lord Cork, the bailiff and other principle inhabitants of Frome to have the performing troop removed from the streets and that the assault charge, 'was begun by Box's kicking the man's drum to pieces as it was beating in the street!' The assault was dismissed but Saunders was given seven days for vagrancy. Hiscox is shown as paying the rates until 1793 after which the property ceases to be mentioned as an inn. The town map of 1813 shows the premises in detail with a forecourt for carriages and a yard or garden at the back. The site became Dodge's furnishers and was rebuilt again in the 1950s for Kelsey's the bedding and house furniture shop. This old painting from 1888 has just caught the corner of its former location on the

92 The scene in 1888

extreme right with the cart outside.

1774 Frome Gets New Vicarage

Lionel Seaman was a well-connected local man who became vicar of St John's in 1742 and laid the foundation for his new vicarage in 1774 but in1758 he became Archdeacon of Wells and left the town. Local antiquary John Skinner made a sketch of the building as it was in 1821 but it has been greatly remodelled since that time.

93 1821 Sketch of the Vicarage by Rev John Skinner

94 The remodelled Vicarage in 2023

1785 Jeremiah Cruse Survey.
In September of this year surveyor and mapmaker of Longleat and Bath, Jeremiah Cruse conducted a survey on behalf of Lord Weymouth, *A Particular Account of the Number of Families & Inhabitants within the Parish of Frome Selwood*. This careful and detailed record was carried out in conjunction with a Mr Battle and listed the district, name, occupation and property owner of everyone in the parish to a total of 8,185 people.

In 1813 Cruse went on to produce the magnificent parish map of Frome Selwood lately reproduced by the Frome Society

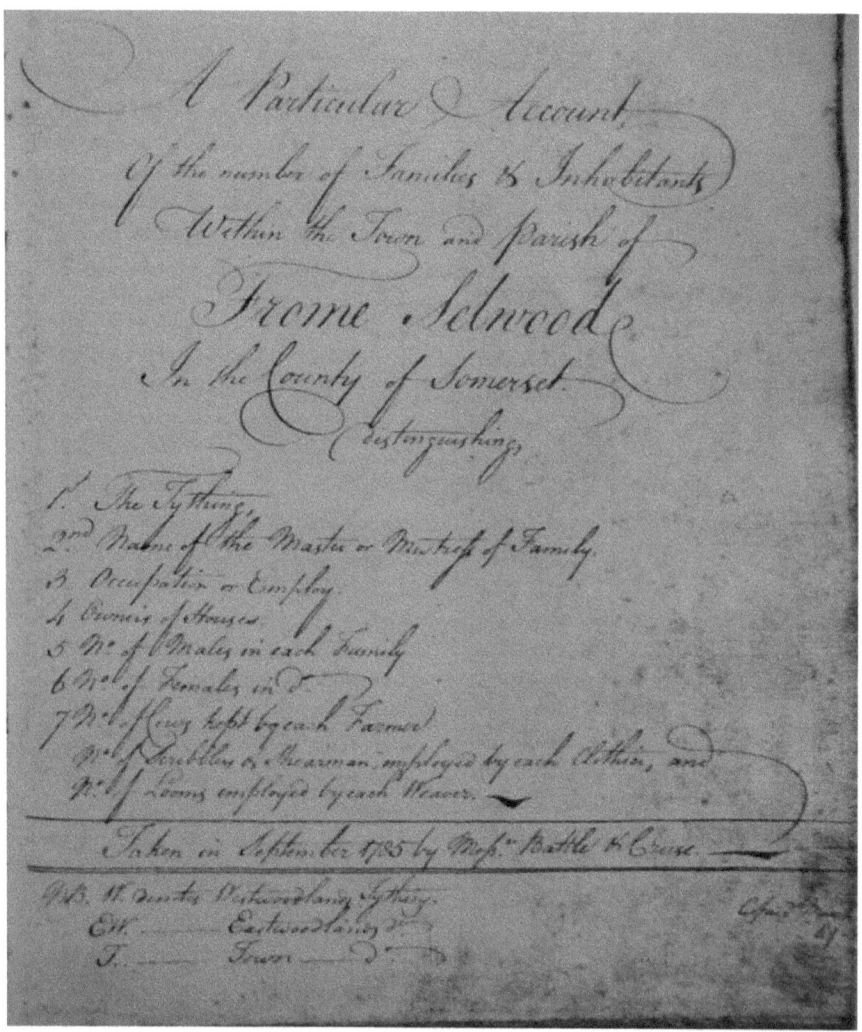

95 Title page of the 1785 Survey

1785 Backsword: Men with Sticks.

Men have probably been hitting each other with sticks since the stone age or before but during the 16th century and into the 19th it evolved into a spectator sport. Matches took place under various names in different places including 'cudgel play' or 'singlesticking' and at one time it was second only to wrestling in popularity. The rules, if they can be called that, were quite simple. The two opponents stood close together, facing each other and without moving their feet bashed each other as hard as they could on any part of the body above the waist. The winner was the first to draw blood from the head of his opposite number, (producing a flow of more than one inch in length).

In Frome we called it 'Backsword' and its first appearance in print dates from the *Bath Chronicle* of September 1772 when a 'handsome silver cup 'was awarded to the winner and, 'good encouragement will be given to the gamesters'. There is no mention of location other than to say that the event will take place during the races and be played between nine and one o'clock.

On the 1774 map of the town it is quite clear that a stage was set up

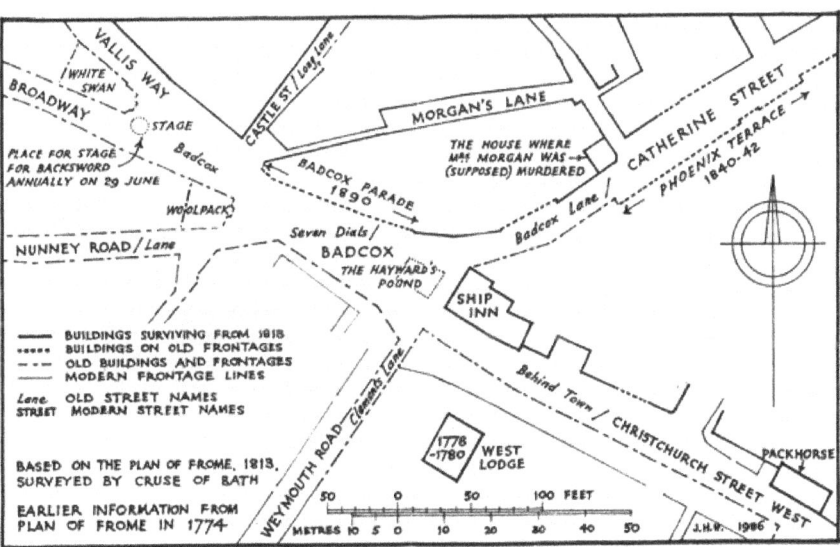

96 Map of the area c 1813 (Dr John Harvey)

annually at Badcox near the White Swan where the car park is today and eleven years later again in the *Bath Chronicle* there was the following advertisement:

> **Frome, Somerset**
> To be PLAYED for at BACKSWORD, at Frome, on Thursday and Friday 15th and 16th of September, TEN GUINEAS each day; likewise, One Shilling to be

given for every blood drawn, and Half-a-Crown to him that draws it. Persons breaking three heads to quit the stage, and the tiers, if any, to be settled by the claimants.

As the greatest proficiency in this Ancient Science seems to be warmly contended for by the counties of Wilts and Somerset the subscribers to this play, wishing for a fair and equal trial to which the palm is due, propose, if the Wiltshire men attend on Thursday and play with padding, that on Friday the Somerset shall play them without it; but if the Wiltshire men should not attend Thursday and play as proposed, the gamesters shall be padded Friday; likewise, should there be any of this subscription remaining on Friday evening, it will be played for Saturday morning as the gentleman present agree

Frome seems to have been something of a centre for this noble art. In the summer of 1786 the town hosted a match featuring 'Somerset against all England' for a wager of ten guineas each day. By 1808 the sport was known as Single Stick and an exhibition in November of that year

afforded such excellent sport as perhaps was never before witnessed. It may be truly said, it was a feast for the amateurs of that manly exercise. The principal object of this match was to afford the Somerset and Wiltshire gamesters an opportunity of displaying their prowess. The Wiltshire men, after losing six heads declined for the first day all further contest and the Somerset men, of course, secured that day's prize.

When the day was done Somerset emerged as clear winners and it was

97 'The scouring of the White Horse' 1859 Thomas Hughes 1859 (William Linton artist)

reported that,

> Both parties uniting, spent reminder of the day with goodwill and harmony. Every accommodation was provided at the different inns for the numerous and respectable company that attended amongst whom were some of the first characters from the counties of Somerset and Wilts.

This ancient and noble sport would make a wonderful addition to events at the Frome Festival and it would be fascinating to see if Somerset lads can still carry off the prize by bonking the noggins of those Wiltshire softies.

1791 population of Frome 8,105

1792 Abraham Crocker Starts His Press

Abraham Crocker, Frome resident and schoolmaster at the Blue House set up a small printing press at the school in about 1792 so that he could supplement his income of a mere £20 per year as well as instruct pupils in the art of printing while producing small leaflets and posters for local people. The project took off and he and two of his sons John and Philip moved into the business of printing books and selling through their own shops in Cheap Street and Bath Street. The first surviving example of their work is a poster from December 1792 entitled, *Resolutions of the Frome Loyal and Constitutional Society*. This was a declaration of loyalty to the king and a call to arms against sedition and the 'inflammatory suggestions of evil designing men.' A meeting was chaired by local magistrate Thomas Horner of Mells and signed at the bottom, FROME: PRINTED BY J AND P Crocker.

98 Abraham Crocker (Frome Museum)

Abraham and his sons were prolific artists, surveyors, cartographers, printers and book sellers with the father writing books on English grammar, mathematics, and cider, while Phillip became chief steward at Stourhead.

1797 The Cutting of North Parade.
The road improvements made under the act of 1757 made the town something of a bottleneck with its narrow medieval streets and so a new way out of town was created, - North Parade.

99 Toll Gate North Parade (Frome Museum)

100 North Parade looking south from the railway bridge.

Whereas the present road leading from Frome town bridge to a place called North Hill is very narrow and incommodious for travellers and carriages… a new road is to be made from the said bridge to join the present Turnpike Road leading from Frome to Beckington at or near search place called North Hill, and if it was given to the said trustees to pull down and remove certain houses and buildings now standing and being in sight of the new of approach road.

1799 In Praise of Cyder.
One of the undoubted joys of living in the West Country is that on a hot summers day one can never be far from a refreshing pint of dry farmhouse cider straight from the wood. Long ago it was produced by most farmhouses and many individuals who took it into the fields to slake their thirst as they toiled away in the sun, often taking it as part of their wages, but today things are quite a bit different.

101 Pressing the cheese

In one sense cider is its own worst enemy. Stronger than beer, easy to drink and very cheap it was a firm favourite with lads experiencing delights of the public house for the first time. They would spend every little, get drunk very quickly, then pick a fight or throw up. Not the sort of custom that a landlord would encourage. Proper cider is about 6% and needs to be treated with respect. Decades ago the landlord found a solution in offering a drink which was pasteurised, diluted, bland and made undrinkably fizzy with the addition of carbon dioxide. In recent times this once glorious drink suffered even more indignities by being saturated with sugar and mixed with various fruit juices, a monopoly which seemed to have taken over the town's pubs for a while in recent years.

Today there is only one pub in Frome that sells a decent pint of real cider and that is the Lamb & Fountain who serve an excellent pint of Riches. In Stony Street there is Andy's Micro pub which sells a variety of different ciders including Roger Wilkins's, possibly the greatest of them all. The Blue Boar in the Marketplace has Cheddar Valley on tap which is very drinkable but not what you would call real.

Things were very different in 1799. Abraham Crocker, produced a small book which he called, *The Art of Making and Managing Cyder deduced from Rational Principles and Actual Experience.* He circulated his knowledge amongst a few friends who were so impressed that they persuaded him to set it out in book form. Crocker had a good friend, John Cranch, artist and polymath who was a supporter of the newly installed American government and a fellow of the American Academy of Arts and Sciences. Cranch was related by marriage to John Adams the second president and Crocker's little book was enthusiastically supported and promoted in that country – possibly Frome's first export to America.

The 40 page book describes in detail the best kind of cyder producing apples including, 'Captain Nurse's Kernal, Barn's Door, Staverton Red- Streak and the Broad-Nosed Pippin' none of which you are likely to come across today.

The process sounds like a simplicity itself, but of course there's a lot more to it but these are the basics. Shake the tree and when the apples drop they are ready for use. Mix whatever varieties you choose and basically smash them to bits until you have a large pulp known as a 'cheese' this is then pressed until the juice runs out which is left to ferment and placed in open vessels for a couple of days before being placed in barrels and left for the winter. At the beginning of March, the cider should be expected to be bright and clear and ready for bottling. Crocker concludes that, 'By the month of July following, the Cyderist will find himself possessed of a grateful, lively, sparkling and exhilarating liquor, highly delicious to the palate and congenial to the human constitution, fit for princes and the best of their subjects to regale themselves with'.

As well as a schoolmaster and author Crocker spent much of his career as a land surveyor, artist and valuer. Little is known about his private life but his portrait hangs in Frome Museum.

A decent drop may still be obtained from:-
Roger Wilkins. Wedmore 01934 712385
Hecks. Street 01458 442367
Riches. Highbridge 01278 794537

6
THE NINETEENTH CENTURY

1801 The population of Frome was 8,748

1803 Keyford Asylum Opens.
The Keyford Home or Asylum was built between 1789 and 1803 when it opened. It owed its existence to Richard Stevens a tanner who having no family left his

102 A print of 1804 (Wellcome Collection)

fortune to be used for charitable purposes and this was the result. It was run as two separate establishments providing homes and education for young girls destined for domestic service along with a home for old men. The establishment

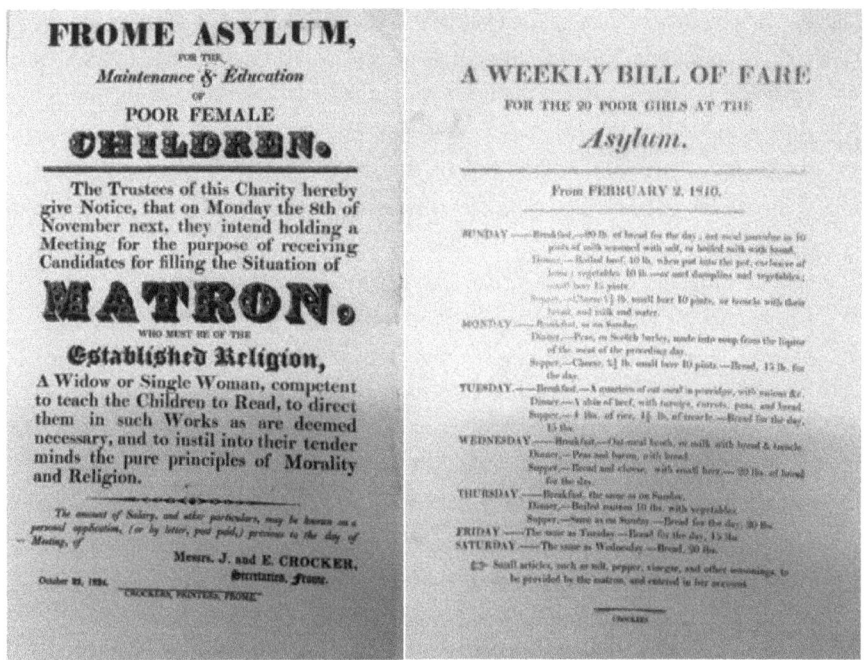

103 Feeding the Girls in 1810 (Frome Museum)   Matron Required 1824 (Frome Museum)

stood at the corner of Culverhill and what is now Steven's Lane named, of course, after Richard. This fine looking building was demolished in 1956.

1808 The Tremendous Storm.
Although climate is high on the agenda today a Frome pamphlet from 1808 reminds us of some remarkable occurrences in the past. On 29 April 1697 Dr Halley, of comet fame, reported that a storm of thunder, lightning and torrential rain estimated as two miles in breadth, and 60 miles in length passed over Cheshire & Lancashire, small animals were killed, trees split, horses and men struck down. Some hailstones were said to be five or six inches in circumference. Other storms hit Hertfordshire five days later where the shower of hail contained stones measured from 10 to 13 inches across, 'some persons were killed their bodies beaten black and blue'.

Abraham Crocker, schoolmaster at the Blue House in Frome, author, scientist and surveyor wrote a pamphlet about it and continued,

> Superior, however, to either of these both in extent and grandeur was the Somerset storm of 15th July 1808. Standing as I did, about two miles from

the eastern limits of this most memorable tempest, I had full opportunity for viewing and contemplating those magnificent volumes of electric fire which exhibited themselves every three or four seconds. In less than two hours this thundercloud had increased to a vast magnitude extending its lurid bulk over the horizon from SW to NE and its thickness I found by observation and computation to be nearly a mile. Its progress was nearly 70 miles and its average breadth about 8 miles so that the space of earth over which it was suspended and its progress was not less than 550 square miles. The lightning exhibited flashes vastly extended and highly vivid which darted it every direction the thunder was one incessant roar by which 1000 reverberations was continued incessantly on the ear, the whole continuing its awful splendour from hour to hour.

The following morning was fraught with intelligence of the devastations caused by a tremendous shower of hail which fell at the time such as the oldest man living in our country had not remembered. The hailstones were extraordinary in both size and form some small as a pea and others larger than an orange some round others broad, polygonic angular or crenated.

So fascinated was Crocker by this event that he wrote to many respectable and learned persons in surrounding villages and towns discovering that the storm had entered the country at Milborne Port where it divided into two

104 The Great Storm

branches northward and westward. In places the thunder was 'one incessant roll for three hours without a moment's intermission and it seemed that all the magazine of heaven had been opened and all its artillery let loose upon us'.

At Bruton some of the hailstones measured more than seven inches round, at Stratton a house was flattened, at Shepton Mallet a horse was killed at Mells Park more than 3000 panes of glass were broken at the manor house fields of wheat, oats and barley were entirely destroyed as were all garden vegetables all roads strewn with leaves and branches of trees. At Ammerdown small animals were killed and the roofs of buildings materially injured with glasshouses utterly demolished.

Frome had no newspaper of its own at that time but the *Coventry Herald* records the storm as coming after a day of the most oppressive and excessive heat and at its height 'The inhabitants was so much alarmed at this extraordinary visitation that they trembled for their lives; and few of them, to use their own expression, expected to behold of the return of day.' Further up country at Horsley in Gloucestershire a fireball fell upon the house of a Mr Whittard throwing down a considerable part of the roof and entered a room where his ill niece was in bed. 'It perforated the wall, split one of the rafters and forced its way through to the dwelling underneath before darting out through a window without any of the parties sustaining the smallest injury other than dread occasioned by their perilous situation'.

1809 George III Golden Jubilee

Frome on 25 October 1809 was ushered in by the ringing of bells and flags and streamers waving from the steeple. To gladden the hearts of the aged sick and poor a subscription had previously been made upwards of £100 to be distributed in beef bread and money to such poor as were of the age of his Majesty upwards oppressed by the hand of sickness. Of the former class there what about 300 who received 4½ pounds of beef, a quartern loaf and a shilling each; the remainder of

105 The King's Statue Weymouth erected to celebrate his Golden Jubilee 1809

the subscription was distributed among the sick and poor families of the town. The day concluded with bonfires and fireworks.

John Bumpas 1887

1810 The Cutting of Bath Street

Strange as it may seem today, before 1812 Bath Street didn't exist at all and the main way out of Frome Market Place was up Stony Street and then either left

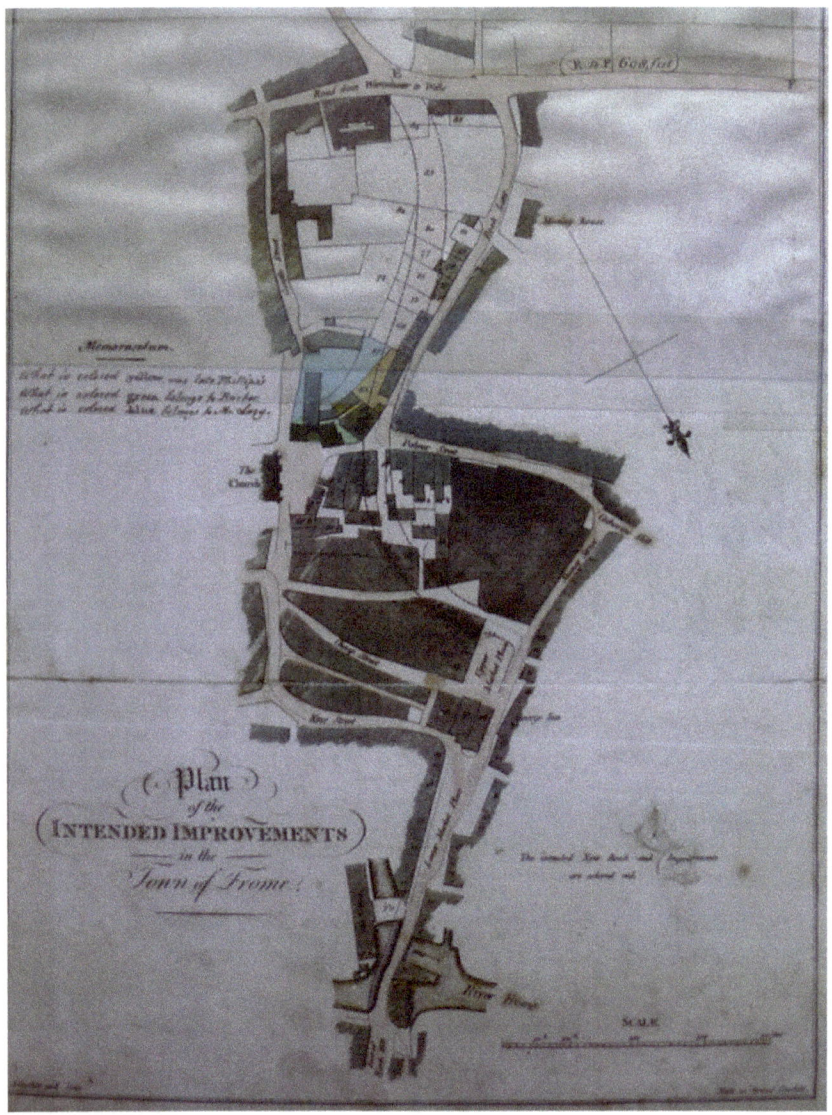

106 The Cutting of Bath Street

along Palmer Street and into Rook Lane or right up Catherine Hill, all narrow dark and badly maintained roads.

The Market Place was divided into two halves, Upper & Lower with a pub opposite, and within a few feet, of the door to the George alongside two other shops making the whole centre of the town cramped, dirty and dark. One of the prime movers behind the radical improvement to the town's layout was Thomas Bunn a local solicitor and philanthropist who had visions of transforming the town with sweeping Georgian terraces like Bath. His description of the area to be cleared says it all,

> I have counted three dung hills from one spot in a principal thoroughfare. In the very centre of town near the Market Place, and principally in a place called Anchor Barton, was such an accumulation of dung hills, slaughter-houses and tallow melting houses as is undescribable. The principle thoroughfares were narrow lanes. That I might not mistake, I have measured some of them which remain. In the wider parts they are, including two footways, about 16 feet 7 inches; in the narrower parts 13 feet and 11 feet 10 inches.

Reflecting on the improvements many years later he wrote:

> This town was one of the worst if not the very worst in the county of Somerset the thoroughfares, mere lanes, so narrow that carriages could not pass each other without ascending the footways. In 1810 after being conversed about improvement the previous 20 years act of parliament was passed for that and other purposes. Union Street was adopted as a model for convenience, the space for the carriage road being 26 feet and each footway 7 feet in the whole 40 feet. Of the spread of the new roads have been made at Frome. There was necessarily an excavation of the road 16 feet in depth. 'The dunghills and other offences were removed, and on the banks of joining the new road shrubs and flowers were planted. The architecture was improved particularly the west front and gateway of the parish church designed by Sir Geoffrey Wyattville.

The new road involved the demolition of this slum area which was dominated by the Anchor Inn pub standing partly where number 4 Bath Street is now, the one with the two Ionic columns at the front which date from 1836.

Some of the remaining ancient cottages can still be seen behind the large cedar tree past the rear entrance to the Old Bath Arms on your right as you go up towards Christchurch Street. The cottages which faced them across the narrow Rook Lane were swept away by the new road - a job made easier

107 Bath Street in the 1860s

by the fact that the freeholder of most of the land required was the Marquis of Bath of Longleat which is how the road got its name.

Amongst the new buildings along the road is the impressive gothic screen which leads to St. John's church. Between that and the church itself was a jumble of decaying slums including a pub called the Bell standing almost next to the church door, all demolished to make way for the road and give a more imposing view of the church. Still impressive today and little altered apart from its shop fronts, Bath Street has some fine buildings, well worth a stroll on a sunny afternoon.

1812 Vandalism at St John's.
In 1812 a most appalling bit of vandalism was committed. The Bell Inn and certain cottages had dominated the churchyard to its detriment for many years. The parishioners called in James Wyatt, an architect who was employed to build the stables at Longleat, and, in addition to clearing away the inn and cottages, a new west wall was built of clean white Bath stone. Goodness knows what he was thinking, possibly removing the gothic to fit in with a clean 'Georgian' classical look in line with Bunn's dream. Luckily it doesn't seem to

108 St John's Encased by Wyatt

have stayed for very long. The estimated cost of the new west front was £842 10s., and the sum voted for the gateway which led into Bath Street was £136.

1813 Drunken Colliers Riot

> A serious riot took place at Frome, on Friday last, in consequence of a drunken set of colliers endeavouring to obstruct the peace-officers in the performance of their duty. The Earl of CORK, Col. HORNER, Colonel JOLIFFE, and Mr. IRELAND, being in Frome at the time, and on the bench as Justices, endeavoured to enforce their authority; but were attacked most furiously by the mob, who rescued their prisoners, and proceeded to unroof the gaol, which they partly effected. The Frome cavalry and infantry were called out, who succeeded in securing six of the ringleaders, who were strongly escorted to Ilchester gaol. Colonel JOLIFFE received a violent blow, which cut through his hat; Mr. IRELAND, Lord CORK, and Colonel HORNER, received several blows. In consequence of this outrage, the Frome and East Mendip Cavalry have been ordered out on permanent duty, as these deluded men have threatened to revisit Frome.

109 Newspaper report of the riot

1813 Jeremiah Cruse Map.

Jeremiah Cruse, 1758-1819, was a leading professional land surveyor and mapmaker in the late 18th and early 19th centuries. Working from premises in Bath, Cruse was a native of Rode and a resident of Frome. He had long-standing connections with Thomas Thynne of Longleat, 2nd Marquess of Bath, whose estate included about half of the parish of Frome Selwood in Somerset.

In 1813 Cruse undertook a survey of the whole parish for Lord Bath, producing a large and highly detailed map for the Longleat estate. At the request of the parish he produced a copy of the map for St John's church in the same year. The map is huge and measures over 11 feet high by nearly 7 feet wide, covering 6.7 by 4 miles. The original belongs to Frome but is stored at the Somerset Heritage Centre for safe keeping and has now been reproduced in its entirety as a full coloured atlas by the Frome Society

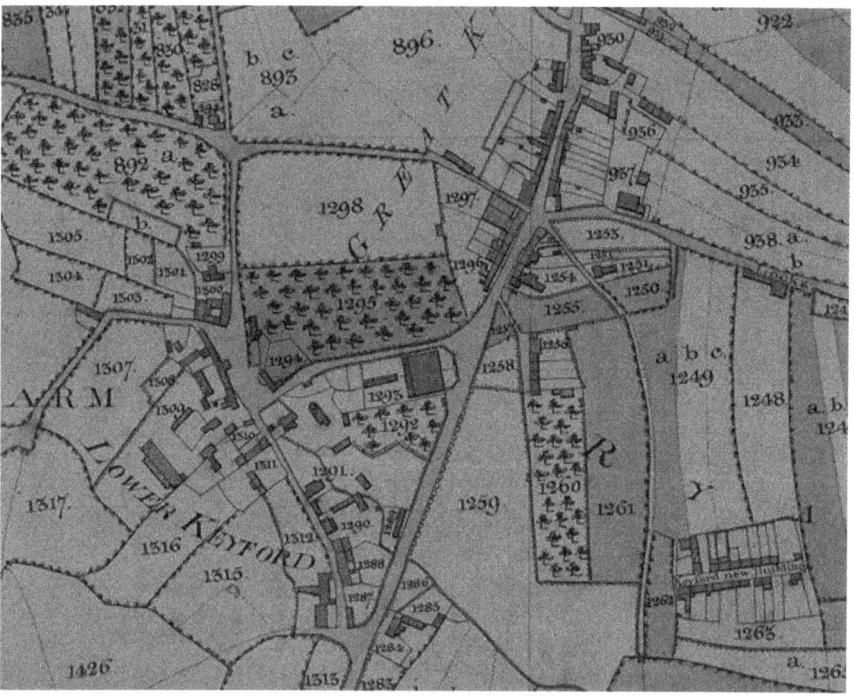

110 Keyford Section of the 1813 Cruse Map (Frome Society)

1814 pillory last used in the Market Place

1816 Potato Riot.
A riot lately took place at Frome by an immense assemblage of poor persons, in consequence of an advance in the price of potatoes; the civil power was utterly disregarded, and the military, with difficulty, could disperse them.

1818 Assembly Room and Covered Market Opens
The building on the corner of Market Place and Cork Street was constructed in the kitchen garden of local philanthropist Thomas Bunn. According to reports in the local newspaper its upper room measured 48ft by 24ft, was an incredible 24ft in height and connected to the George Hotel. The Assembly Room opened on 14 August 1818 with a public dinner and quickly became the scene of many concerts and society balls including a notable banquet to celebrate the coronation of William IV.

111 The Assembly Room & George in 1906

The original ground floor was initially the meat market, situated at the end of the Upper Market known as the 'shambles' where cattle were killed and butchered. Sometime later it became the Market Hall, until 1875 when the new one was built down beside the river, (now the Cheese & Grain) The old undercroft was sold off to become a branch of Stuckey's Bank, and after a number of mergers and takeovers it eventually became the National Westminster until its closure in 2023. In the 1970s the bank took over the Assembly Room as well, subdividing the magnificent space and using it as offices, its last function was a civic reception held on 16 March 1974 to mark the end of the Frome Urban District Council.

1819 Cockey of Frome.
The Cockey name has been prominent in Frome history since 1682. The family were influential in clock-making, bell-casting, iron founders and agricultural engineers. Lewis Cockey was an active member of the town and a church warden but it was his eldest son Edward who formed Edward Cockey & Sons in 1819. Their main business was focussed on an ambitious range of iron and brass castings including street furniture, bollards, drain covers and parts for the newly invented gas street lighting. This diversified into gas production, purifiers, gas holders, scrubbers and condensers, enabling Cockey to produce and supply gas lighting to Frome as early as the 1830s. The family quickly became proficient in gas engineering and safety and by 1851, employed 76 people. The stylised streetlamps, that are unique to Frome were created

112 A Cockey lamp head by St John's Churchyard

with the advent of electricity in 1904 when the existing gas lamp standards were converted and adapted with JW Singer & Sons' art nouveau leaf designs. In the same year ten arc lamps were erected on Portway, Badcox, Bath Street and North Parade. Little is known about the design or the fate of these lamps and there are between 70 and 80 Cockey lamps left many not listed and in a sad state of repair.

1821 New Shops on Frome Bridge
The bridge over the River Frome and into town is one of less than a handful in the country with buildings along its length the others including Pulteney in Bath and Lincoln This alone marks it out as special and worthy of attention.

113 Frome Bridge Buildings in the 1990s

The buildings you see today were constructed in 1821 and replaced a parade of shops dating from the 18th century which included a pub, The Full Moon, and some dye houses taking advantage of the river. The precise date of these shops is uncertain but may possibly pre-date Pulteney Bridge.

1823 Broadcloth Weaver's Strike

> a special meeting of the magistrates for the division of Frome was held yesterday when ten weavers were committed to Ilchester gaol for refusing to finish work they had taken for the purpose of manufacturing, an example, which it is hoped, will operate beneficially on the minds of a number of working-class people who it appears, have been misled and intimidated by the desires of a few desperate and dishonest characters into thinking that they should have more coin for their work. The greatest praise is due to the magistracy of the neighbourhood for their continued and prompt exertions in reconciling the differences between these men and their employers and for their vigilance in preserving the peace in the town. Colonel Horner appeared early in the morning as head of six troops of North Somerset Yeomanry to give assistance to the civil powers that be.

114 Van Gogh's home weaving frame 1884 (CC)

1825 Frome National School, Bath Street.
In 1819 organisers of the Frome Sunday schools met to consider the building of a National School in the town. This organisation had been founded in 1811 and was based on teaching by the, 'monitorial' system whereby a small group of promising pupils were taught the lesson by a master and then repeated what they had learnt to groups of younger pupils. By this method a master could control anything up to 1,000 pupils in a large school. The site chosen for the new building was at the top of Bath Street with land purchased from Lord Bath. A committee of local worthies was assembled and an architect chosen, Mr W Finden of Bath. Although little known, Finden, was a successful architect who had carried out some commissions in the Melksham area a few years before.

What he produced was a delightful, graceful building in the gothic revival style which opened on 26 September 1825 with the boys on the ground floor and the girls and infants on the floor above, each having their own entrance. Income was to be generated by fees and donations. There was a headmaster and headmistress paid £50 and £35 respectively and children could only be admitted by subscription or approval by a board of visitors. Subscribers of three guineas per annum could recommend nine children and so on through a

115 Edmund Crocker's 1825 sketch of the National School, Bath Street

sliding scale to half a guinea for one child. Parents were to send their children regularly and punctually at 8:45 am and 1:45 pm with school finishing at 4 pm and there was to be an annual exam. In 1826 the children were, 'regaled with roast beef and plum pudding', but by 1829 this had changed to cold meat. The school was to have a very religious bias and opened on Sundays for further religious instruction. The girls were instructed in needlework and it seems that they got paid by taking in items determined by the school supervisors, but work for the parents and charities was to be done, 'gratis'.

In 1830, 'Mrs Crocker made some pies which were given to the children at Whitsuntide, less than half the weight, on average, of the pie she sent as a pattern. It was agreed that she be paid 2 1/2d per pie rather than the agreed 4d'.

In 1885 the girls were removed to Christ Church School and the boys from that establishment moved here. It served its purpose well until it closed as a full-time school in 1934 when it was superseded by the new St John's School in Christchurch Street East. The building was used for school meals until 3 November 1965 when it finally closed. Without a use the fabric of this delicate building which had been supported internally by a steel framework, deteriorated still further, unfashionable and unloved despite its elegance it fell victim to the destructive zeal of the 1970s and was finding demolished in 1974 to be replaced by a terrace of low-rise houses – The Maltings, totally out of keeping with the rest of the street, after the fashion of the time but now softened by some bushes and foliage.

116 The Maltings today

1826 William Cobbett. 1763-1835 A Noble Agitator

A most remarkable man at the turn of the 18/19 century was William Cobbett, perhaps not as widely appreciated as he once was, his story remains quite extraordinary. He was born in Surrey in 1763 son of a farmer. He began work as a farm labourer before taking the stagecoach to London and working as a clerk at Gray's Inn during which time he taught himself English grammar. He became a soldier reaching the rank of sergeant major. He went to America and earned a living by teaching English to the French and opening a bookshop there.

His experiences with corrupt officers during his time in the army drove him towards political campaigning and he championed the English against the revolutionary Americans. Returning to England he produced pamphlets, magazines and newspapers in support of a variety of radical causes, spending two years in prison for his troubles. Nonetheless he continued publicising and publishing his often eccentric views, writing in favour of Catholic emancipation and although he voted for the abolition of slavery after becoming MP for Oldham he maintained that British factory workers were also slaves and treated more harshly than those in the West Indies.

By far his best known book was *Rural Rides* which was published in 1830. In September 1826 he took a post-chaise from Warminster and came to Frome where he saw upon entering the town,

between 200 and 300 weavers, men and boys, cracking stones, moving earth, and doing other sorts of work, towards making a fine road into the town. I drove... through the principal streets and put up at one of the inns. This appears to be a very small Manchester, though it does not contain above 10 or 12,000 people, but it has all the flash of a Manchester and the innkeepers and their people look and behave like Manchester fellows. I was, I must confess, glad to find proofs of the irretrievable decay of the place.

117 William Cobbett in about 1831

These poor creatures at Frome have pawned all their things, or nearly all. All their best clothes their blankets and sheets, their looms, any little piece of furniture that they had and that was good for anything. Mothers have been compelled to pawn all the tolerably good clothes that the children had. In case of a man having 2 or 3 shirts he is left with only one. This is a sort of manufacture that cannot very well come to a complete end; still it has received a blow from it cannot possibly recover.

The population of Frome has been augmented to a degree of one third within the last six or seven years... new houses in abundance, half-finished new gingerbread, 'places of worship' as they are called, great swaggering inns; parcels of swaggering fellows going about with all vulgarity imprinted upon their countenances and with good clothes on their backs. I found the working people at Frome very intelligent, very well informed as to the cause of their misery and not at all humbugged by the canters whether about religion or loyalty. When I got to the inn I sent my boy back to the road to tell one or two of the weavers to come to me at the inn. The landlord did not at first like to let such ragged fellows upstairs. I insisted, however, upon their coming up and I had a long talk with them. They were very intelligent men and had much clearer views on what is likely to happen then the pretty gentlemen of

Whitehall seem to have; and, it is curious enough, that they, the common weavers should tell me, that they thought that the trade would never come back again to what it was before.

1827 The Notorious Howarth Brothers
Soon after midnight in the early hours of Monday 6 August 1827 two lads observed three men, acting suspiciously in a timber yard, as they approached the men ran off. They woke the owner, Mr Oxley, who grabbed a lantern and carving knife and the three made their way towards the wood store where they found a considerable amount of timber had been stacked outside ready to be carted away.

Oxley discovered a 'very powerful ill-looking fellow' secreted amongst some bushes with a drawn sword in his hand. The villain attempted to escape, cutting backwards with his sword but was pursued by Oxley who fought sword against carving knife, until the fellow cried for mercy and threw down his weapon. The arrested man turned out to be a millwright named George Howarth who had been residing in Frome for some years. The constables searched his home at the old nunnery in Keyford and found it literally crammed with stolen articles of every description among which were;- elegant dresses, books, barrels of gunpowder, pistol bullets, Bath stove grates, a dog house, iron bars, new beams, sets of scales, new timber boards, chains, bags of hops, casks, velvet pulpit cloths and cushions, nails, screws, blocks, every kind of labouring and gardening tool, silver spoons, a tanned cow hide, leathers, earthenware, new brooms, servant's liveries, bags of feathers, etc etc. The velvet pulpit cloth and cushion had been stolen from Christchurch in Frome some six years ago. Howarth's brother Ralph was also apprehended and his house searched revealing a variety of articles some of which have been identified by persons from whom they were stolen.

The culprit was taken to the Blue Boar public house for the purposes of having his wounds attended to, but managed to escape on Tuesday night by leaping from a window seventeen and a half feet high into the water and gaining the opposite bank. Howarth was described as about five feet ten inches tall aged about 55 of strong muscular form; dark complexion with rather coarse prominent features and several wounds on the head, the hair of which is shaved off, a stab wound on the left side; and a cut across the upper part of the nose which last were inflicted at the time of his capture. He had an imperfectly cured fracture of his left leg slightly above the ankle which has made his leg slightly crooked and his gait slow and down looking, his feet were about twelve inches long and proportionately large, his features regular; grey eyes with thick bushy eyebrows nearly meeting over the nose. He spoke with a North Country dialect and was by trade a millwright like his brother but has worked as a sawyer, and a ships carpenter. A reward of fifty guineas which was offered immediately for his recapture was soon doubled to one hundred.

Brother Ralph's house was raided at the same time as his brother. He too lived an outwardly respectable life as a master millwright and member of the Methodist Church. Stolen goods were found on his premises and he was sentenced at the Bridgwater Assizes during August 1827 to two terms of seven years transportation for stealing a gun and a sack from William Baily in Frome along with other items. Ralph was sent to the prison hulk *Captivity* at Devonport on 17 September 1827 to await transportation to Australia.

George was eventually re-captured and returned to Frome where things weren't looking to good. The following day, Thursday 6 September 1827 he examined by the magistrates at the Assembly Rooms above the George Inn in Frome. He was strongly secured in irons as he faced the various charges:

1. Stealing oak planks from the store room of Mr. Oxley.
2. Cutting and maiming Mr. Oxley.
3. A Robbery at Christ Church in Frome.
4. The theft of 13 blankets from the parish manufactory at Frome

For a period of 16 years the Howarths had been inhabitants of Frome during which time they have been in the constant habit of committing robberies of the most daring and criminal nature without awakening suspicion. Sheep and calves had been stolen from fields, joints of meat from butcher's shops, cloth from factories and even sacrilege had been committed by them. Frequently, innocent persons had been arraigned on suspicion of committing these crimes. They maintained the respect of those who knew them to such an extraordinary degree that to have spoken a word derogatory to their good name would have been considered an insult.

Howarth's trial at the assize court in Taunton took place in April 1828. He appeared dejected and stood with his arms crossed in a 'declining posture' with his head held very low, when asked to plead he raised his head slightly and said in an almost inaudible voice, 'Not Guilty'. The jury was asked to consider its verdict on all the charges arising from the Oxley burglary and found him guilty on most of them. George was sentenced to be transported for fourteen years on the burglary charges and the learned judge did not mince his words.

Under these circumstances your life is forfeited to the laws of your country and from what I have ascertained of the catalogue of your offences you have certainly been a wicked and desperate character; the sentence of death must therefore be recorded against you; whether you will suffer the penalty due to your crimes depends on the recommendation to be made to his majesty. I would not have you flatter yourself that your life will be spared, but prepare yourself to meet the contrary event. If, however the former should be the case it will be for the purposes of ridding this happy country of you for the term of your natural life.

His Lordship ordered sentence of death to be recorded against the prisoner who appeared unmoved at his fate and departed from the dock without betraying the least emotion.

It seems that the trial judge, Justice Littledale, had at some point 'humanely interposed on his behalf' presumably seeing some good in him, he received a reprieve and was sentenced to be transported for life. On 8 September 1828 at the age of 58 he was moved to the prison hulk *Captivity* at Devonport to await transportation, the very place that brother Ralph, 49, had been sent to one year before, possibly he was still there and the two brothers sailed off together.

> George Howarth, the notorious burglar, was tried on Thursday, for cutting and stabbing, with intent to murder, Mr. John Oxley, of Frome, on 6th Aug. last. Jury found the prisoner *Guilty* on the 6th and 8th counts. His Lordship was of opinion that being acquitted of the 6th count, he was convicted only of the misdemeanour. As the 6th count only applied to the Vagrant Act, and the 8th count was too general, he should respite judgment till the next Assize.—— The prisoner was then put on his trial for Sacrilege in stealing a surplice, velvet cushion, looking-glass, &c. from the parish church at Frome Selwood. The articles, although found in Howarth's house, were stolen from the church at Frome in the year 1821; and his Lordship observed that there had been such a lapse of time between the period the crime was committed, and the time when the property stolen was found in the prisoner's house, the Jury had better acquit him of that charge, as the property might have gone through several hands. He was consequently *acquitted*.—— The prisoner was then arraigned for stealing 28 blankets, the property of the parish of Frome Selwood; and subsequently for stealing 10 pieces of oak plank from Mr. Joseph Oxley, of Frome Selwood. On both charges he was found *Guilty*, and sentenced to *Fourteen Years Transportation*.

118 Bath Chronicle 10 April 1828

1830s The New Face of St Johns.

This beautiful lithograph of the West front of the church by C Burton a London artist and engraver shows Wyatt's screen of 1813 as well as the old front. Note the cultivated garden to the left now sadly abandoned. Picture courtesy of Rev Colin Alsbury.

119 The West Front by C Burton 1830s

1830 Unemployment in Frome.

A report in the *Bath Chronicle* of 25 February, 1830 is headed 'Distress at Frome' and continues: 'There are at present in Frome no less than 5,000 paupers receiving weekly pay which reckoning on an average of only 1/- each amounts to £250 weekly or £13,000 yearly. The weekly payments to the casual poor at the close of last year amounted to £89.15. 1½ or £4,667.6.6 yearly: since which time there has been a considerable increase. This class of paupers consists of able-bodied men, driven from their usual employ through the stagnation of trade. Many of them were not long since ratepayers and considerable manufacturers but are now subsisting on parochial relief at the rate of 2/- each and 1/- each child to the amount of 6 children and 1/6 to their wives weekly. On 4 March, 1830, the *Chronicle* recorded that the Bishop of Bath and Wells had presented a petition to the House of Lords from the inhabitants of Frome complaining of distress:

> the state of misery to which the labouring part of the population was reduced was unparalleled in the history of the country. In several parts of Somerset, the persons who received relief from the poor rates exceeded in number those who paid the rates. . . (with) his own eyes had seen numbers of his fellow men yoked together like oxen & engaged in drawing coals from the pits in that neighbourhood [Bath].

They bore their suffering, he said, with a constancy and fortitude deserving of the highest praise.

1831 Emigration to Canada.
So great was the poverty in the 1830s, trade having been declining for some years, that the church vestry attempted to solve the problem by encouraging people to emigrate to Montréal in Canada. The first group of 85 left Bristol on the steam ship *Airthry Castle* in March with their fares paid by the vestry hoping to save money on future welfare payments. The following year about 140 people went. Each head of family was given £1 with which to establish themselves,

> The parish of Frome had been placed in difficult circumstances for many past years. The trade, which had collected a numerous population, having declined, could no longer support them; and thousands have become dependent on the poor rates, and charity for their daily subsistence. The higher classes have paid great attention to their wants and comforts; and they have shewn, by their conduct, that they are sensible of the kindness of their more affluent neighbours. Every usual expedient has been resorted to improve the condition of the poor:-large public subscriptions the cultivation of land; the establishment of manufactories; the improvement of the system at the parish workhouse; spade agriculture; the alteration of roads; and a variety of other things.
> Thomas Bunn

1831 Gas Lighting Comes to Frome
Lewis Cockey came to Frome about 1685 from Warminster and established a bell foundry. The family business diversified in the 18th century and in the

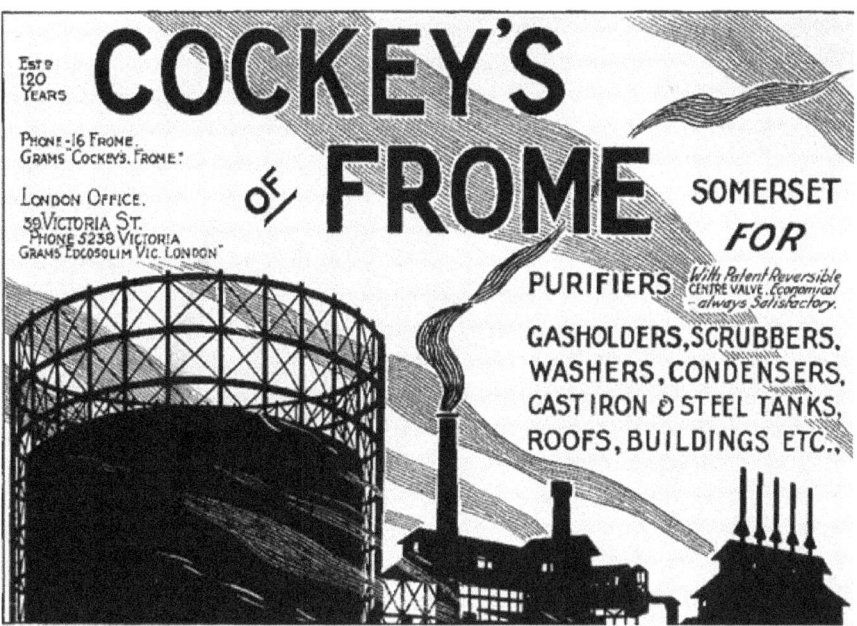

120 Ad from Modern Gasworks Practice 1921

early 19th began casting for the gas industry. Edward Cockey (1781-1860) became a successful iron-founder and in 1816 founded the firm which by 1851 was employing 76 men and boys in the Palmer Street foundry as Edward Cockey & Sons. In 1886 they became a limited company and in 1893 the works moved to the Garston area of the town. The Frome Gas Company was founded by Cockey and the town had had gas street lighting as early as 1831. They made delightful 'art nouveau' gas light standards with a leaf pattern many of which survive to this day around the town. The firm was wound up voluntarily in April 1960 leaving a legacy of bollards, drain covers and lamp standards many displaying the name.

1832 Reform Act & Election Riots.
Parliamentary Elections were held for the first time in the new borough of Frome created by the recent Representation of the People Act and polling was to take place on the 10,11, and 12 December 1832 at the George Inn. Many small landowners, tenant farmers and shopkeepers were able to vote for the first time and in Frome the total electorate was increased to slightly more than 300 out of a population of 13,000. Thomas Sheppard, a retired London banker who lived on Hampstead Heath in London was the first to put himself forward and it was assumed by most that he would stand unopposed. In fact,

121 A Rather Premature Cartoon of the Time

he had been canvasing for the candidacy since the year before in anticipation of the reform bill going through but within a few weeks Rear Admiral Boyle, brother to the Earl of Cork who owned large parts of the town and surrounding countryside expressed an interest in opposing him and announced his intention to stand. Both expressed their support for the principles of reform; in fact, they had appeared together along with many other local dignitaries including Sir Thomas Swymmer Mostyn Champneys at a mass meeting in Frome's Market Place on 15 May.

It is something of a truism that history is written by the victors and it is certainly true of the events of December 1832. Things started well with much celebration and excitement, a whole ox was roasted at Pilly (Willow)Vale and a massive bonfire built in the Market Place where the Boyle fountain now stands, it was said to have been as high as a house and upon it was placed a huge coffin to represent the end of the old electoral system. The Market Place was crowded with people, flags and bands of music. The normally accepted view of what happened during the election itself was the subject of a long report issued by Thomas Sheppard and his supporters, *Narrative of the Frome Riot,* from December 1832. This is their version of events (abridged)

The Narrative of the Frome Riot.
About nine o'clock in the morning about forty men on foot, bearing Mr Sheppard's favours; and without weapons of any sort, came to Cork Street; and stood quietly near, but not on the steps of the hustings, to protect the approach to them.

Sir Thomas SM Champneys, Bart. arrived at half-past ten, accompanied by many hundred men and boys, many of them armed with bludgeons and cudgels; most of them were on foot, but they were attended by men on horseback. A great number of them wore *white* ribbons, white sashes, or cards inscribed with Sir Thomas Champneys' name; many of them appeared not to be men of Frome; some of their bludgeons and cudgels were loaded with lead.

Some of this party immediately assailed Mr Sheppard's men, and drove them away from the hustings. The men wearing white colours, then took possession of the ground round the hustings, and of the Upper Market Place, in front. Soon after, Mr Thomas Sheppard, attended by a very considerable number (perhaps about five hundred) of supporters, none of them with sticks or weapons of any sort, entered the Lower Market Place. A large party of men, both foot and horse, wearing white colours, then moved from the hustings to meet them; and those who preceded Mr Sheppard's carriage were stopped, and driven back by this party, who formed across the road; Mr Thomas Sheppard and his friends near him were then assaulted by some of the other party, who opposed his entrance to the hustings, and tore part of his and some of his friends' coats from off their backs.

On Mr Thomas Sheppard's attempting to speak to the meeting, his voice was drowned by clamour; and, during the whole day, he was unable to obtain a hearing; stones and other missiles were also thrown at him.
Sir Thomas Champneys then addressed the Assembly at great length, and was loudly cheered by his party, and not interrupted by Mr Thomas Sheppard or his party. Violent and unprovoked attacks were made on the friends of Mr Thomas Sheppard, several times during the morning.

So much violence was shewn by the riotous party, that a requisition was made to the magistrates to swear in special constables, magistrates of the Division of Frome, commenced swearing in Special Constables, at the George Inn, at six o'clock in the evening.

Shortly after, a numerous and formidable mob of men with white colours, many of whom were recognized as the men who attended Sir Thomas Champneys, on his entry, armed with cudgels, bludgeons, and stones, without having received any provocation by the magistrates or special constables, forced their way into the George Inn and made an attack on the magistrates and constables.

After a very severe conflict, which continued more than an hour, and in which several on both sides were very seriously wounded, and the inn much damaged, the assailants were driven out, and the door strongly barricaded: but the threats, as well as the conduct of the Rioters were so formidable, that the magistrates sent for a troop of the Seventh Regiment of Dragoons, stationed at Trowbridge, who arrived most promptly that night.

In the mean while the inn was beset by the mob, who deliberately broke the windows, and excluded any public communication with the persons within. During this and the following days an attack on Mr George Sheppard's house being apprehended, three hundred men were kept by Mr G. Sheppard at his house, at Fromefield; and also about two hundred men divided between Mr Byard Sheppard's and Mr William Sheppard's houses, and at their different factories,– these men, after Monday morning, never going to the Market-Place, or interfering with what was going on there, or in any degree with the election, otherwise than guarding these buildings, except about fifty who were sworn in special constables.

The polling commenced, and Sir Thomas Champneys' voters went to the polling-room, from Cork-Street, through the Market-House, which the room adjoined; and Mr Thomas Sheppard's voters went, at first, through the George Inn front door, but about eleven o'clock being interrupted from going that way, went by a private way through the Crown Inn, and a sort of cellar of the George. About noon, an attempt was made by the mob to force an entrance into the George Inn, which was resolutely resisted by the special constables; several of them suffered from the bludgeons and stones of the assailants. The George Inn front door was now again barricaded.

Many more of the inhabitants of Frome were sworn in as special constables during this morning. Mr T Sheppard did not appear on this day at the hustings or in the town, as his friends and the magistrates wished to prevent any cause of additional excitement in the mob.

A little more than an hour after the polling was over, the Dragoons again entered the Town, and remained until about half an hour before the Polling commenced on the next day.

Before the polling commenced on Wednesday, Captain Edgell, one of the magistrates, stated at the hustings to Sir Thomas Champneys, that some of the special constables were armed with firearms, and that, if such violence took place as on the preceding days, they would be ordered by the magistrates to fire.

On the Wednesday, Mr Sheppard, at the request of the magistrates and his friends, again abstained from appearing in the town. By about ten o'clock, on this day, Mr Thomas Sheppard had polled 163 Votes, which were more than half of the whole number of persons having votes; so that Sir Thomas Champneys, even if he should have polled every other voter, could not have been returned. Indeed, the original number on the List of Voters being 333, and many having, since the list was printed and before the election, been struck off from change of residence and other causes; the number of 163 was considerably above half. At about eleven o'clock, the mob commenced deliberately pelting at the remaining windows of the George Inn; and continued doing so for an hour or two.

Between one and two o'clock pm a large body of the mob wearing white ribbons and favours, and shouting,' 'Champneys for Ever,' made a most furious attack on the Crown Inn, (through which, and the George Inn, Mr Sheppard's voters passed to the place where the poll was taken,) for the purpose, it is supposed, of forcing their way into the George Inn, which having been barricaded since the attack on the preceding day, could only be approached this way.

The mob effected an entrance; and proceeded to demolish the bar: one of the special constables had his arm broken, and others were most seriously injured, in attempting to oppose them. The magistrates then ordered the special constables, about twelve of whom were armed with carbines, to make a sally from the George through the Crown and repel the assailants. They succeeded in driving them from the Crown, and in clearing the space in front of that Inn, and of the George as far as the hustings. The magistrates read the Riot Act, and were both struck with stones; and seeing that the mob closed again upon the special constables as they returned, and continued to assail them most violently with stones and brick-bats (some of which were thrown from the hustings,) and that many were already seriously wounded, ordered them to fire. The special constables, many of whom were bleeding profusely from the wounds received from the missiles, determined to preserve coolness and self-forbearance, still remained patient under the showers of missiles which were striking them. They retreated to the Crown door, where they were again attacked by the mob in the same manner. At length, after repeated warnings to the mob of the consequences of their conduct, and earnest entreaties that they would disperse, three or four shots were fired. By these shots two men were severely wounded, one of them below the knee, whose leg it was found

122 The George Hotel 1905

necessary to amputate, and the other in the thigh. These two men had taken an active part in the riots: we are happy to find that they are both likely to recover. The Troop of the Seventh Dragoons, who on the previous day had marched to Beckington, were recalled, and entered the town about three o'clock, which necessarily stopped the poll.

Shortly after the firing Sir Thomas Champneys went home, and in the evening sent in his resignation to the returning officer, requiring that the poll should be opened *pro forma* on the following morning, giving notice that such resignation was without prejudice to any proceedings he might institute as to the election being illegal. The poll was opened on the Thursday, but no votes were tendered; and at the close of the poll the numbers were as follows:
Mr T Sheppard.... 168   Sir T Champneys ...100 —— Majority for Mr Sheppard.... 63

On the Thursday morning the polls re-opened but there were no more votes and to his apparent astonishment Champneys lost the election to Sheppard by a majority of 63, 100 votes to 163. The Dragoons were recalled for the night once more and Sir Thomas left to return to Orchardleigh with a large party of followers.

1838 Frome Workhouse Established

Frome union workhouse was built by 1837 on the south side of Weymouth Road. The construction cost £5,400 to accommodate 350 persons. It was built in a Y plan which included a central hub with three radiating accommodation ranges with exercise yards for the various classes of inmate. There were 26,236 people within its range at the 1831 census, a vast number for such small accommodation. From 1904 birth certificates for those born on-site were shown as having been born at 29 Weymouth Road to save them from disadvantage later in life. The building became Selwood Hospital until 1988 when it was developed for housing.

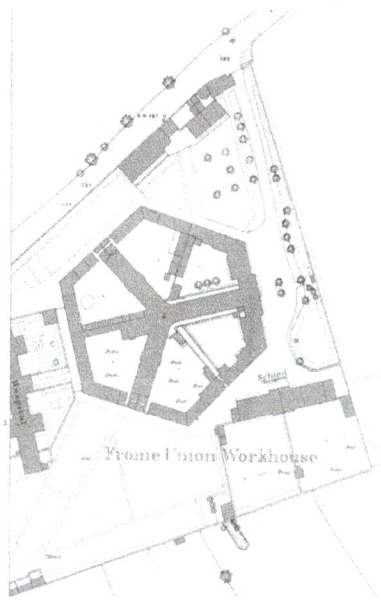

123 Frome Workhouse on the 1886 O/S Map

124 The Workhouse Tramps Quarters in 2016

1844 The Frome Literary Institution.
The following article by local historian Derek Gill appeared in the *Frome Journal* for 20 August 1981. (abridged),

The Frome Literary and Scientific Institution was founded in 1844. It could have been established 30 years earlier for at the annual meeting of the Frome Reading Society, on the 25 March 1814, a Literary Institute was proposed, and largely supported by one who could later claim to be the father of the 'Lit', Thomas Bunn. On that occasion, and again in 1836 the idea failed to gain enough support and it was not until 1843 that the suggestion was made once more. Thomas Green of South Parade who kept a diary, now in Frome Museum, wrote,

> January 23, 1843
> Attended a meeting at the Vicarage, (Saint John's) for establishing a lecture room and museum, after some discussion it was agreed to make a commencement and Mr John Sheppard promised to give £10 and Mr George Sheppard and myself £5 each if £200 were raised besides an annual 20 shillings.

In those days few bought daily newspapers, the only source of national and international news were the London papers which cost 5d, apart from *The Times*, which, with the largest circulation was 7d. At that time there was a stamp duty and no reduction in the price of papers could be made until its abolition in 1855. A reading room as was envisaged, would enable more people to read a newspaper. One of the first priorities was to find suitable premises. Thomas Green continued,

> January 30 1843
> Attended a meeting at the Vicarage on the proposed Library and Lecture Rooms and went with Mr J Sheppard to look at two houses in Bath Street.

> October 16 1844
> Met Messers Dusautoy, Daniel and Giles at the house in Bath Street and Vicarage Street to ascertain the best suited for the library.

Eventually the Masonic Hall in Palmer Street next to the present Old Bath Arms was chosen and served the Society for over 20 years. In February 1843 Thomas Bunn had called a meeting inviting steps to be taken for the establishment of the library. A letter had been printed and circulated inviting members and dated 1 February at Frome Vicarage, it read in part

> It has been thought desirable to commence the formation of a library, and to hire apartments, where books and other collections may be kept, and used, as well as to obtain from members of the proposed Society or from others, occasional literary and scientific lectures. 17 people gave their names to this appeal headed by Thomas Bunn then in his late 70s.

The Institute was to be managed by committee including a president, vice president, treasurer, secretary and other members. A subscription of not under 10 shillings was to constitute a member, whilst one guinea admitted a member to the private reading room for a year. There was to be no religious or political controversy. The rooms were to be open from 10 am until 9 pm daily except Sundays.

Amongst the first members were most of the local leading citizens and clergy, Nonconformist and Anglican. However, there was controversy in 1853 when the Roman Catholic priest Fr Ward applied to join. Only two members supported him and they resigned in protest at this intolerance. Initially 110 people joined the society. A programme of lectures on travel, natural science, philosophy and other classics was prepared, occasionally, a paid lecturer was to be booked for variety. On January 24 1845 the inaugural lecture was given by the Rev. Richard Meade, Thomas Green wrote of the occasion,

> Attended introductory lecture of the Frome Literary Institute at the George Assembly Rooms, delivered by Mr Meade at 7 o'clock. The room was full and the lecture admirable. Mr John Sheppard made a good extempore speech afterwards, as did Mr Horner of Wells, the president, Mr Dusautoy proposed that Mr Meade's address be published.

The society became a centre for most of Frome society and did more than any other institution to promote the social and intellectual progress of the town, and immediately became the most popular according to contemporary witnesses. Over 600 visited it in its first year. Some of the members who had wandered to all parts of the world sent back interesting communications. Many prominent citizens of Frome donated items to the society, among these the Rev John Horner of Mells gave 253 books and a collection of minerals, corals, shells, insects and fossils as well as 100 cases of birds and two cabinets of medals and coins.

125 The 'Frome Lit' in 1904 (Frome Museum)

John Sheppard gave 108 books Mr Wickham of North Hill House gave 90 books, and Thomas Bunn a set of Chippendale chairs and 14 objects for the museum. In fact, the latter was far more generous. He bequeathed all his pictures and objects of art. Shortly before his death he executed a deed of gift of Monmouth House and other property which he hoped would in enable the society to build permanent premises on the southside of Christchurch Street West opposite Rook Lane House, where he envisaged a grand crescent to rival Bath.

His 'Temple of Science', the centre of the crescent, was to be the premises of the Institute and would have been a real architectural ornament to the town standing in such a prominent position. Unfortunately, his gift was so complicated in its conception that after his death his trustees were unable to proceed with it. A perusal of the wealth of books in the library of the Institute shows the breadth of vision and interest of those early members. Many bear the surnames, Sheppard, Bunn, Horner and other leading families of the time. One I examined recently originally belonged to Mrs Elizabeth Rowe, poet who lived in Rock Lane House until her death in 1736. The flyleaf records her gift of the book to Eleanor Sheppard and successive Sheppard owners until the last, John, who gave it to the, 'Lit'.

At the inaugural meeting of the Institute, the President of the Royal Society, the Marquess of Northampton, was made patron and the Rev JSH Horner, rector of Mells, was elected president.

By the 1860s the society had outgrown its first premises and a long struggle followed to find more permanent ones. Thomas Bunn's dream never materialised and it was thanks to the generosity of a local cloth manufacturer, John Sinkins, of Wallbridge House that a final solution was found. He financed the building which now graces the corner of Bridge Street and North Parade at a cost of several thousand pounds. The Institute therefore, finally acquired spacious premises which provided a fine reading room, museum and a flat for the caretaker.

At the annual meeting on 8 October 1869 members spoke in glowing terms of their new premises. John Sinkins died shortly before, but he had lived to see his creation completed. At that time there were 3,197 books listed in society's catalogue with 107 members.

1840s WW Wheatley, Artist.
WW Wheatley (1802-1868) was a watercolourist famous locally for his depictions of the streets, churches and antiquities of Frome and surrounding area. He lived in the village of Rode for many years before moving to work in Bristol and Bath. He carried out many commissions for patron of the arts George Braikenridge who engaged him to produce numerous illustrations for Collinson's *History of the Antiquities of the County of Somerset.*

In 1848 he produced what is perhaps one of his most famous paintings,

126 Wheatley's view of Cheap Street 1845

the clipping of Rode Church. The villagers would hold hands, and form a circle around the church facing inwards and dance around the building. The dance ended with a huge shout which was supposed to drive away the devil for another year. The ceremony continues to the present day.

1840s The Infamous Maggs & Sparrow Gang.

The Maggs-Sparrow gang, named after its two leaders, were responsible for most of the crime committed in the town during the late 1840s and early 1850s. So much so that one newspaper reported that they 'infested the neighbourhood' with their nefarious and, for the most part, nocturnal activities. Their modus

127 The Clipping of Rode Church 1848 (Alastair McLeay)

operandi usually involved the stealing of food stuffs – bread, cheese, potatoes – from local shops or neighbouring fields in order to feed their dependents. William Maggs, had a family of thirteen–many of whom would follow in their father's footsteps with varying degrees of success.

The situation turned more sinister when Maggs and Sparrow, along with fellow villain Robert 'Frome Bob' Hurd, stood trial accused of the rape and murder of a fourteen-year-old girl on a farm at West Woodlands. The murder of Sarah Watts remains unsolved; she was left at home while her parents went to market and her body was discovered when they returned. Several members of the gang were arrested and charged but evidence was rather slim as none of them were convicted.

Although found 'not guilty', it was not long before they were back to their old ways, first Sparrow, then Maggs, found themselves in prison for theft. Both men were condemned to transportation for life, although neither was destined to leave these shores and served their time at home. Maggs died before his ship could set sail and Sparrow served out most of his sentence behind the walls of Dartmoor prison. With their leaders incarcerated, the remainder of the Maggs-Sparrow gang tried to carry on but their activities were short lived. One secret to their success was uncovered when, with these later arrests, a large bunch of skeleton keys was found in their possession which could open just about any premises within the town.

128 Dartmoor Prison where William Sparrow served his time

1850 the Railway Station Opens.

In October 1850, the steam age came to Frome with the official opening of Frome Railway Station. This event was the culmination of a five-year process that had begun with an Act of Parliament in 1845, giving the go-ahead for a line between Westbury and Frome. This led to the Wilts, Somerset & Weymouth Railway Company being formed to undertake its construction and Isambard Kingdom Brunel appointed engineer of the line. It turned out to be a bumpy ride, as an economic depression near the end of the decade put paid to the company and the Great Western Railway – its parent company – took over responsibility.

This was in in March 1850 and work on the line continued over that summer, with a station for the town being planned and erected. The building was designed by T. R. Hannaford – an assistant of Brunel – and took the form of a timber train shed with two platforms and accompanying tracks being covered by a roof. The line was officially opened on 7 October 1850, with a special train excursion to Oxford. According to one newspaper account the people of Frome seemed less than enthusiastic about this leap into the modern era.

The journalist dispatched to cover the proceedings, and expecting to record the usual rejoicing, returned with a 'blank note-book'. There were no church bells to sound the coming of the railway, the newspaper bemoaned, no flags to wave the engine past, nor even a cannon discharged to mark the historic event. In hindsight, the said reporter left too soon, as there was a

129 Frome Goods Yard with the Malthouses in the background

celebration of sorts that evening. A dinner took place at the Crown Hotel in the Market Place, which was situated next to the George, although even then many of the fifty invited guests failed to turn up. One of those who did make

130 Frome Station today. (Frome Museum)

an appearance was local businessman and magistrate, John Sinkins. He had several reasons to be cheerful, most of which were financial. He had owned much of the land the railway line from Westbury had been built on, and so had made a lot of money from the process.

Despite its somewhat muted start, the line has served the people of Frome well during the subsequent 170 years, especially after the line to Weymouth was completed six years later. Although these days only a single track runs through the station – at one time there were two – the building itself is now Grade II listed and a rare example of its type still in operation.

1852 Madam Carlyle is not Impressed.
Thomas Carlyle (1795 –1881). British essayist, historian, and philosopher from the Scottish Lowlands and a leading writer of the Victorian era, exerted a profound influence on 19th century art, literature, and philosophy. Whilst travelling from Paddington his wife Jane, described as one of the finest letter writers of her time, was forced to make an unscheduled stop over at Frome; she describes her experience in a letter to her husband.

Frome is a dull dirty looking place, full of plumbers; one could fancy the Bennett controversy must have been a godsend to it. I saw several inns and chose 'The George' for its name's sake. I walked in and asked to have some cold meat and a pint bottle of Guinness's porter. They showed me to an ill-aired parlour and brought me some cold lamb that the flies had been buzzing around for a week – even Nero [her dog] distained to touch it. I ate bread, however, and drank all the porter; at the charge for that feeble refraction was 2/6! Already I had paid £1.08.06 for the train. It was going to be a most unexpectedly costly journey to me. But for that reflection, I could almost have laughed at my forlorn position there.

131 Jane Welsh Carlyle (1801-1866) –(Public Catalogue Foundation)

The inn and town were so disagreeable that I went presently back to the station preferring to wait there. One of the men… came to me as I was sitting on a bench and remarked on the beauty of the scene, especially some of the scarlet beans that were growing in his own piece of garden. 'Ah, he said I have lived in London and I have lived abroad, I've been here and there back and forwards while I was in service with them who as never could rest, but I am satisfied now that the only contentment for man is growing his own vegetable. 'Look at them beans', he said again. 'Well, tomorrow they'll be ready and I'll be pulling them and boiling them and eating them – and such a taste! No agriculture like that in Piccadilly!' Then he looked sympathising at me and said, 'I'm going to get you something you'll like that's a glass of cool fresh clear water,' and he went away with a jug to his garden and fetched some water from a little spring and a great handful of mignonette. 'There! there's something sweet for you and here's splendid water that you won't find the like of in Piccadilly! I asked him how it was going with Mr Bennett? Huh! I here no complaints but I goes to neither one nor other of them, and follows my own notions. I find agriculture the thing!' He would have been worth £100 to Dickens that man.

I had the coach all to myself for a while; then a young gentleman got in, who did exactly the right thing by me, neither spoke to me nor looked at me until we stopped at Castle Cary......

The controversial priest William James Early Bennett was appointed as the vicar in 1852. Bennett is celebrated for having provoked the decision that the doctrine of the Real Presence is a dogma not inconsistent with the creed of the Church of England.

1853 Rossetti School Opens (briefly)

A plaque on the wall of the three-storey building in Brunswick Place, Fromefield records that Christina Georgina Rossetti (1830–1894), poet and member of

132 Rossetti School Building, Fromefield

the Pre-Raphaelite literary movement, ran a school in this building from April 1853 to March 1854 after which the Rossetti family returned to London.

1856 Frome's First Police Force.
In the first half of the 19th century the administration of justice in the countryside was pretty much the same as it had been for hundreds of years. Many people were suspicious of a full-time police force fearing that the government might use it to oppress them but as crime grew so the need for a properly organised force became more urgent. It was also time to do away with the old parish constables and night watchmen who were inefficient and largely part time. The first police force in England was formed in London in 1829 by Sir Robert Peel and in 1835 local government in England was reformed compelling all London boroughs to form their own force. In 1839 counties were permitted, but not compelled, to form their own police forces in rural areas and this was made compulsory in 1856.

The first organised police force made its appearance in the town in 1856 stationed in the former Eagle Inn at the bottom of Church Steps where the hideous yellow brick building is now. Contemporary reports declared it to be a temporary station where 'a constable is always on duty night and day'. They did not stay long as by the census of 1861 Edward Deggan aged 32 the Superintendent of Police was living at the newly built police station in Christchurch Street with his wife and daughter. Originally from Bristol Deggan had served in Westminster and Axbridge before being promoted and moving to Frome in 1860 for a salary of £120 per year plus allowances.

Also living at the station on census night were five constables in their 20s and three prisoners one of whom was Richard Hoddinot aged 37 a journeyman* butcher, the other two being general labourers. Sadly, their crimes are not recorded on this occasion but Mr Hoddinot was apprehended for poaching in Buckland Dinham in 1865 and got three months hard labour.

The brand-new police station, a large sprawling building in the Gothic taste standing on Golden Knoll provided not only accommodation, but the magistrates court with a large hall and four cells for the prisoners. Although newly built soon after the new act Frome was pipped at the post by a station completed at Kilmersdon in the summer of 1857, 'the first police station in the

---

* journeyman is a term which applies to a tradesman who has finished his apprenticeship and is a qualified craftsman entitled to work on his own account. It has nothing to do with travel. The word comes from the French *journee* meaning 'a whole day' as he was entitled to charge a daily rate for his work.

133 The Frome Police Station and Courts of 1857

County of Somerset' built by Aubrey Catley general builder of Mid-Norton.

In 1856 the Somerset Constabulary consisted of 260 men under the direction of Chief Constable Valentine Goold, 1 Deputy Chief Constable, 4 Superintendents, 12 Inspectors, 20 Sergeants, 90 first class constables, and 132 second-class constables. The annual cost of this hearty band of men was estimated to be £13,778.

During his long career Deggan was involved in the last stages of the notorious Sarah Watts murder when in 1861 a Joseph Seer confessed to the murder of a young girl 10 years before. His confession was dismissed as being deluded and the case is still unsolved. In 1867 he investigated the murder of Martha Britten by her husband George on their farm at Woolverton.

Deggan retired in 1885 on a pension of £84 2s at the age of 55 after 28 years in the force, he died in Somerset Road at the age of 71 in 1899

1861 Murder at Buckland Dinham.

In August 1861 Uriah Greenland and Byard Greenland, Uriah's uncle and fellow labourer William Millgrove were returning home from Codford to Buckland Dinham, a distance of about 20 miles, after spending the previous week bringing in the harvest. At Warminster they were picked up by a brewer's dray and taken to a pub called the Black Boy at Corsley where Uriah, who was a parish constable, got involved in trying to stop an argument amongst some locals and was knocked down a couple of times before the party managed to escape, and with money from the harvest in their pockets they moved on to the Live & Let Live on Portway in Frome until around 10.45 when they set out to walk the remaining three miles to their homes in Buckland Dinham.

During the journey, as they approached the turnpike on Coal Lane, Murtry, Uriah said to Byard, 'You might as well put the reckoning to rights," meaning that he should sort out their various small expenses including train travel and food expenditure while they had been away; it seems that the pair had paid towards Byard's fares and upkeep. They agreed, and laid their scythes and reap hooks down beside the road to sort the money out. It seems a strange time to do it, by the roadside in the dark when all three lived only a short distance up the road but that is what was agreed nonetheless.

Byard claimed that the Uriah owed him 18 pence for some damage done to a gun and would not hand him any money until that matter was resolved. Uriah agreed and there seemed to be no argument between them but suddenly Byard lurched towards Uriah who fell back onto the road exclaiming, "Oh Bill! He has been and hit that knife into I"! Millgrove claimed later that he did not see a knife despite being about two feet away from both parties. He picked the injured man up and laid him against the bank saying to Byard, "Thee has been and done it now then", to which Byard replied, "Canst thee swear that Bill?" "I can," replied Millgrove.

Millgrove went to find the nearby toll keeper who found Byard cradling Uriah with his arm around his neck and felt for his pulse which he found to be extinct. Millgrove then set off for Frome to find a policeman and the toll keeper to fetch his daughter leaving Byard alone with the body.

134 A traditional scythe in use

When they returned Byard asked them to examine the scythes which were encased in wooden sheaves and the reap hooks bound with straw; one scythe had a point projecting from its cover but there seemed to be no blood upon it. Byard said to Gane, "I had those (two) scythes on my shoulder and Uriah ran against them".

Next at the scene was Dr Benjamin Mallam the surgeon who arrived to find Uriah still propped up against the bank. He examined the body and found that he had been stabbed through the chest. By now a policeman had arrived and sat with the deceased while Mallam examined the scythes with a magnifying glass but could find no trace of blood. Mallam recruited a local farmer with a truck and hurdle to transport the body to the Globe Inn public house in Vallis Way, Frome.

Byard was charged with murder and tried at the assize court in Taunton. After hearing all the evidence and Byard's improbable story, the jury retired for about ten minutes and 'amidst the most breathless silence' the foreman said, 'We find the prisoner guilty of murder but we recommend him to the mercy of the court, believing that he did not premeditate the murder.'
The jury cited the lack of motive or any financial gain and it seems that Byard had suffered some brain injury many years before possibly causing him to commit impulsive acts and that the only point at issue between the two men was Byard's attempt to seduce Uriah's wife the previous spring. Uriah seemed able to let it go but perhaps Byard's mental state left him seething with jealousy, rage and embarrassment over the matter.

The death sentence was commuted to transportation for life and Byard sailed off to Western Australia where, after being granted parole in 1867, he married and continued his work as an agricultural labourer before dying of natural causes in 1879.

1864 Skimmington Riding
This little tale comes initially from Gare Hill. In 1864 James Elliot, Francis Smith, Henry Wheeler and John Way were up in court for committing a breach of the peace. From the evidence of a woman named Elliot and her son, it appeared that the defendants and many more locals had paraded through the village over a period of three nights with images designed to represent Mrs Elliot's daughter and a man named George Stone who, it was alleged, 'broke the moral law'. In other words they had been caught in a compromising position before marriage to the strong disapproval of their fellows.

The errant pair got off lightly. 'Skimmington Riding' was a custom dating back many centuries, an activity that went by various names and took various forms but the object was always the same – to ridicule and cause embarrassment to someone who had offended the moral sensibilities of their community -to cause the public humiliation of the victim under the eyes of their neighbours. The custom is known from early medieval times mainly in the west country and probably pre-dates less exciting forms of community punishment like the pillory or the stocks.

In this case George and his lady friend appeared only in effigy but in earlier times the miscreant could be set astride a long pole carried by two men while the villagers followed on behind laughing, shouting and jeering to the accompaniment of 'rough music' or the banging together of anything that came to hand from kitchen utensils, bells and whistles to makeshift instruments. In fact the word Skimmington comes from a large wooden ladle which often featured in domestic disputes!

135 Skimmington Riding by Hogarth

Other variations of this jolly custom included being set astride a horse or donkey facing towards its tail and paraded through the streets, their 'crimes' becoming the subject of mime, and theatrical performances along with a litany of obscenities and insults. Often the parade would finish at the house of the offender and could be applied equally to either sex, from nagging wives to errant husbands. In this case the revellers were shown leniency being bound over to keep the peace in the sum of £5 and the practice pretty much died out with the Public Order Act of 1882.

From *Pope's Bath Chronicle* 17 April 1766

Last Easter Monday a numerous -and extraordinary mob assembled in a little parish about 3 miles West of Frome, composed entirely of Rogues, Whores, and drunken Farmer's to execute in effigy their late Overseer. The crime laid to his charge was that he had made it a standing rule during the time of being in his office, for the father of every bastard child to do something if able, towards its maintenance. Those of the mob of most note, were the hangman, the postilion (as they called him) to the hangman; the devil and the parson. The 'hangman' had been lately taken up for a bastard; the postilion, a nog- headed boy about 10 years of age is the fourth child of a very virtuous single woman. This chaste mother is the bastard of a gypsy and dropped about 30 years ago in the porch of a poor woman as a present to the parish and now lives with a young fellow as it necessary piece of furniture in a little paultry ale-house.

The devil has been a devilish whore master; and the parson's morals stand pretty near on the same footing. These four I am told, were the principle actors, the procession began about 4.00 o'clock, (whilst the vestry was choosing new officers) and those that were not furnished with cow bells, sheep bells, brass pans, frying pans and the like agreeable music were assisted with hooting, screaming and yelling all the way to the gallows, where being arrived and silence demanded the mock parson began to exhort the criminal and the audience in a manner suitable to the occasion, this being finished, the hangman to proceeded to execution. The effigy after hanging a proper time it was cut down and carefully laid in a coffin and then delivered to the undertaker. The undertaker when going off was met by the devil and after a terrible conflict was robbed of his charge.

Thus ended this very ridiculous affair. It is surprisingly no mischief was done as the mob in general were very drunk; but I don't hear of any except the burning of a very good greatcoat of the honest drunken farmer's that lent them his cart and the singeing of the gown and cassock of the mock parson.
(courtesy of Clive Wilkins)

1873 A Bull Goes to Market.

In Frome, on Wednesday last a bull which was being driven to market created considerable annoyance to foot passengers and others by the capers it cut. In one street it entered a garden and but for the promptitude of the good lady of the house would have entered the parlour. "Patronising" a few other residents of neighbouring streets, by a peep in at the front door it passed on but by and by in the most audacious manner ascended the steps leading to the house of the police superintendent, it actually walked into the passage and there - in a glass door in front of the animal - was another impudent looking bull. The newcomer was preparing to test the right of his vis-a-vis to the passage when Mr Supt Deggan appeared at his front door and without hesitation served the animal 'notice - in the form of a blow from a ruler across the nose -to quit.' The visitor retired in haste and sprang over the garden wall into the road. He then called on Mr Bird and without ceremony walked into the yard at the back of the house and remained there for at least a quarter of an hour. He then took his leave but being an extremely high-bred bull the neighbouring china shop was of no interest to him and it was instead the pleasure of the animal to upset a carriage belonging to Mr Parsons, the surgeon. In this he was unsuccessful although the shafts of the vehicle were broken, the pony which the bull tried to toss escaped with only a scratch or two and the occupants of the trap were unharmed. The then-infuriated beast was ultimately secured and taken to the railway station.

1880 Mains Water Comes to Town.
Before this time water was drawn from numerous springs and wells and generally speaking families were left to get it where they could in buckets from public pumps, springs or streams often some way from their habitation. The project had been discussed over many years but one problem had been that many property owners who were quite agreeable to water being supplied by a private company to those who asked for it, were not so happy at the prospect of having to pay through increased rates for water supplied by the local board to everyone and in 1874 the scheme was rejected in a poll of ratepayers by 652

136 Garston Lodge in 2023

to 866 against. This remained the case until it was agreed to provide water from a plentiful spring at Egford. The first building to be connected to a mains supply was Garston Lodge an interesting house of around 1800 built in the style of 'Strawberry Hill Gothic'

By April 1881 a report to the local board was able to state that,

> The first service pipe was connected to the mains on 22nd March, 1880, since which time 204 houses, and 259 cottages have been supplied, also 39 businesses by meter. General satisfaction has been expressed as to the quality of the water. It finds great favour from the fact that a considerable saving is effected in tea and in soap. The supply is abundant. I have tested the springs in the driest weather, and found not the slightest diminution. About twelve million gallons have been used during the year...

1883 Frome's Skeleton Army.
In 1878 former Methodist minister William Booth decided to change the name of his fledgling East London Christian Mission to the Salvation Army with the aim of 'saving souls' mainly those of the poor, destitute or drunk –

137 Confrontation 1883

often to the point of breaking the law. The rules within most towns, including Frome, allowed anyone to march but not to preach, so as to avoid creating an obstruction; something the Salvationists did often. Irritated by their constant preaching and determination to turn the workingman away from his pint, a number of groups set up in opposition calling themselves the Skeleton Army, their aim being to confront and disrupt the Salvation Army's activities.

It was only a matter of time before the two groups turned violent, and in the early 1880s there were major clashes in places such as Sheffield and London. Although there were isolated incidents in nearby Buckland Dinham and elsewhere, Frome managed to steer clear of any large-scale confrontation until August 1883 by which time the town had its own Skeleton Army and according to a local newspaper 'the streets of Frome were in a state of disorder the whole evening.' A major confrontation in the market place was avoided because the Salvationists abandoned their original plan of marching through the town. Nevertheless, this did not deter nearly two thousand men and women from making their way to the Salvationist's barracks in Locks Lane to intimidate them with worse to come the following year when another disturbance culminated in a pitched battle, with the Salvation Army finding themselves on the losing side.

1890 Recollections of Old Man Barter.
Mr Barter recalled his early life during interview from 1890 when he was about 70. The time of his childhood experiences would have been in the late 1820s or early 1830s and coincides with the account of Frome by William Cobbett in his *Rural Rides*.

Barter lived with his wife in an old one story cottage that used to exist in the maze of little streets near the printing works of Butler & Tanner in Selwood Road its front door and a tiny window abutting the street while within it was one large room its back wall giving onto a tiny garden being almost entirely of glass to let in light which with the marks on the wall and roof of long vanished machinery told the tale of its origin as one of the domestic cloth works that had been superseded by the factory system. He was a spare little man of some 70 years of age, and a part of his living consisted of the delivery in surrounding villages of the now defunct *Somerset & Wilts Journal*. Sitting there with his good wife beside an open fire he gave me details of his boyhood life.

> At the age of six he was put to work with other youngsters at the Spring Gardens cloth mill. Hours and conditions being unbelievably harsh. When the

mill was busy they often did not leave the factory from Monday morning until Saturday night, sleeping for six hours from midnight huddled up on piles of wood packs and awakened each morning by the foreman's whip. Not that we always slept that long, for on moonlit nights some of us would slip into nearby fields or orchards to steal apples or turnips or anything to fill our empty bellies. On Sundays they would give each of us a Bible to read which weren't much good as not one in 20 of us could read at all.

7
MODERN TIMES 1900 – 2017

1901 Motoring in Frome - the Achilles.
In the first decade of the 20th century Frome had two rival motor car manufacturers. The Achilles was made, or at least assembled, in Frome by Thompson & Co. at Keyford and Butts Hill from 1901-1908 and was available in several versions from 6-12 horse power at prices ranging from £145 to £300 for the four-seater Tonneau version. An early advert boasted that the Achilles was 'vulnerable only in the tyre' playing upon the legend of the hero of Greek mythology who, for those without the benefit of a classical education, was a hero of the Trojan war and a great warrior invulnerable to wounds on his body apart from the heel where his mother had held him when she dipped him in the river Styx to make him immortal. This gave rise to the term 'Achilles Heel' meaning 'vulnerable spot' still used today.

138 An early example of the dangers of the horseless carriage

Another advertisement claimed that the 8hp version climbed the very steep Westerham Test Hill in Kent in 6.1 minutes which is not that fast when compared with the new Mercedes AMG GT 63 S 4 Matic which, we are told, will go from 0-60 in three seconds, but everything had to start somewhere. The first garage in Frome was Hobbs & Sons next to the Victoria Inn in Christchurch Street East, now the pet grooming salon, from about 1906 during which year one was auctioned by Harding & Co. It was described as having, 'Bucket seats upholstered in leather, a genuine De Dion engine, nine horse power, three speeds, forward and reverse gears, artillery wheels, Michelin tyres 750 x 85 mm, painted red and handsomely mounted in brass complete with an acetylene head, petroleum side and electric tail lamps and all in capital running order.' Bidding was by catalogue priced at two pence.

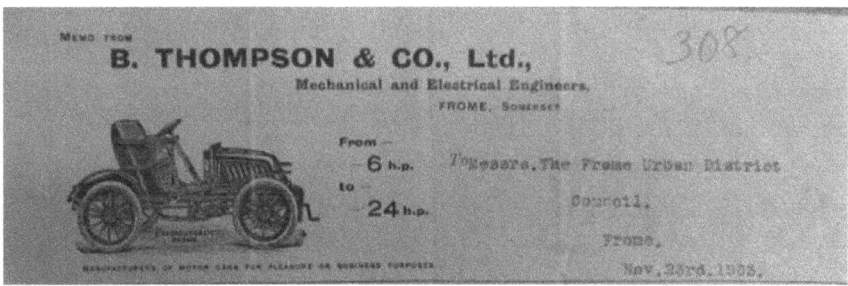

139 Notepaper of 1903

1905 Electricity Comes to Frome.
In the spring of 1900 the newly enlarged Urban District Council met to discuss the question of bringing electricity to the town. Despite the opposition of several influential ratepayers it was agreed that the scheme should proceed and in 1903 a tender by Edmundson's Electricity Company Ltd was excepted at a cost of £20,156 and 5 shillings. Subcontractors included Singer and Sons who were to provide the lamp brackets and builders Hodder & Sons who won the contract to construct the buildings.

Below ground were coal bunkers able to take about 80 tons of fuel; the boilers were constructed by Babcock & Wilcox with the capability of evaporating between 5,000 and 7,000 pounds of water per hour and upon completion it was described as, 'one of the daintiest and at the same time one of those business like engine rooms to be found in or out of the west country'. The original intention of the council was to erect ten arc lamps and about 41 incandescent lamps in the streets but the contractors offered such favourable terms that the streets were lighted by ten, 3-ampere twin carbon arc lamps and 261 incandescent Nernst lamps of 80 CP. The lamps were switched off at 11:30 pm with the exception of the two 40 CP lamps on the arc lamp posts which were switched on automatically when the arcs were switched off. New posts were ordered for additional lamps but the majority of gas lamp posts were utilised and fitted with graceful brackets manufactured at Singer's Art Metal Works.

The contractors also offered to completely wire a house and charged a rental for the use of the installation of £4 and a halfpence per lamp per quarter. Motors and apparatus were also available for hire with Butler and Tanner, Singer & Sons and Gray's sawmills being the biggest users.

Monday 31 July 1905 was scene of a large dinner held at Bull's Hotel in the Market Place to celebrate the establishment of electricity in the town.

140 The works building in 1905

141 A Proud farmer guides his flock in 1910

1914 Refugee Crisis
When Germany invaded Belgium in 1914 Britain stepped in to help deal with one of the major effects of WWI - the large displacement of population. At least 250,000 Belgian citizens took refuge in Britain during the course of the war.

Frome began preparing for an influx of Belgian refugees in September 1914. A national War Refugees Committee (WRC) had been established to source accommodation for those who had fled the country and Frome was one of 2,500 places nationwide that set up a sub- committee to deal with the situation. Meeting at the beginning of September, they passed a motion that 50 refugees be sent to Frome initially and the committee would then judge whether Frome was in a position to take more.

The very first refugees, eleven adults and one child, arrived in Frome on Saturday 5 September 1914, followed by five more on Sunday. They were reported as 'looking worn and sad'. One man's story was typical. He and his wife had to flee having just the clothes they stood up in and some small items which they were able to carry. They had distressing tales to tell of the killing of civilians, and their homes and animals being burned.

Frome residents rose to the challenge of housing the refugees, who were taken into their own homes and in at least two instances had small houses provided for them, at Milk Street and Castle Street. These were furnished and fitted out and were rent free. This was quite a commitment on the part of Frome residents as there was no way of knowing how long this arrangement might last. The thorny question of whether or not the refugees be offered work was raised by the end of the month. It was agreed that work would be beneficial but it was paramount that there was to be no displacement of local labour. If the refugees became self-supporting then this would relieve the local committee of some pressing financial obligations.

Raising funds and support was always going to be a challenge. Locally, benefit performances were held by the Picture Palace, house to house collections were organised, as were weekly subscriptions. Money raised from performances at the Albany went into the fund, as did entry fees from a dance and the 'gate' at a local football match at Badgers Hill. By 23 October 1914 £142/14/3 had been raised. A Christmas tea, entertainment, games and presents were provided for the refugees including a visit by Father Christmas, who seemed to be a novelty to the children. Weekly expenditure went to those who were not billeted in family homes and the rest was earmarked for clothing, the expense of which was particularly high, doctors' bills and incidental expenses.

By 16 October 1914 Frome had a complement of 55 refugees and this number remained pretty constant over the five years.

Newspaper reports about the refugees became fewer and fewer as the years rolled on, presumably indicating their integration with the general population. They were no longer a novelty but a part of the fabric of the town. The last of the refugees left Frome on 3 March 1919. Unfortunately for those returning home it wasn't necessarily a case of happiness and prosperity. Some had difficulty in finding their homes after the destruction meted out by the Germans and found it hard to re-establish their previous lives. There was also some bad feeling amongst those who fled and those who stayed behind and experienced the occupation.

Liz Corfield

1917 Mass Labour Demonstration.

People flocked in their hundreds to Wallbridge and later to Broadway on Sunday afternoon to take part in, or to witness the first great labour demonstration held in Frome. Frome Town Military Band headed a procession of members of the Worker's Union and the National Union of Railwaymen and kindred organisations who were marshalled by the officers of the local Trades and Labour Council. This body had been recently formed to coordinate the various unions and members of those who are not strong enough to constitute branches. Two of them are particularly strong, the Railwaymen's and the Workers Unions, the latter having developed very rapidly.

142 The Demonstration Reaches Portway

Three of the principal officials of the Trades and Labour Council headed the procession, walking in front of the band. Two large silk banners were borne, one being that of the Worker's Union and the other that of the Bath branch of the Railwaymen's Union. Half a dozen females followed the first banner, then between 150 and 200 men-the actual numbers varied from point to point-60 to 70 more women and girls, and nearly a couple of hundred men succeeded the second banner. The route taken was by Locks Hill, Keyford, Christchurch Street, Badcox, Nunney Road, and Portland Road to the Cooperative Society's field at Broadway. Here an open air meeting was held around a lorry which served as a platform for the speakers. The number present was between 2,000 and 3,000 of all classes, women workers and others not employed for wages being in full force. Their banners were displayed behind the lorry.

Somerset Standard 21 September 1917

1918 How the George Lost its Porch.
The George in Frome's Market Place was centre of the town's social and business life for up to three centuries and is mentioned as far back as 1650 but its life has not been without incident.

The fine Georgian building in was the scene of serious rioting during the campaign of Frome's first election after the Reform Act of 1832 and at another election in 1854 when a contest between Tories and Liberals resulted

143 The accident of 1918

in more work for the towns glaziers but this time no one seems to have been seriously hurt.

The old pub had seen use as a ballroom, courtroom and debating chamber, hosted bankruptcy hearings and coroner's inquests but perhaps the saddest event occurred over 100 years ago when on 23 October 1918 a lorry laden with over two tons of scrap metal going from the railway station to Singers & Co took the porch off the front of the building killing Wilfred Hassell a farm bailiff from Wanstrow who was driving a small cart on his way to deliver some apples. Edward Hull, the lorry driver was going down Bath Street and as he turned the corner he saw the horse and float by the hotel entrance, he braked but the road was very greasy and he skidded into the lower pillar knocking it down, crushing the float against the hotel wall and throwing Hassell out of the cart and under the falling masonry.

Dr Harris was quickly on the scene and found the man unconscious and badly crushed with not long to live. He had him taken to the Victoria Hospital where he died shortly after. This startling photograph was taken within half an hour of the crash. A verdict of mis-adventure was brought in by the coroner with no blame attached to either party and a little later his widow was awarded £300 in compensation. The porch was never rebuilt.

144 ... and again in 1968

In May of 1968 history almost repeated itself when a refrigerated lorry containing half a ton of pig carcasses crashed into the same spot trapping one baby in a pram against the pub wall while another was snatched from under the vehicle. Luckily no one was seriously hurt.

1919 Frome Gets its Own Tank.

While most was owed to those from Frome killed in the terrible European war, a great debt was due to those who returned or were unable to take part. Throughout the First World War and after, many individuals and organisations from the town were recognised for their contribution towards the war effort, and in 1919, the year after war ended, Frome was acknowledged for the financial assistance it had provided towards the national war fund, it being estimated that town's populace had donated more than half a million pounds through the Frome War Savings Committee during the four year conflict.

145 Frome receives its tank December 1919

In recognition of this, and to show their appreciation, the town was presented with a Mark IV (female) Tank, No. 231, with two six pounder guns plus machine guns (now thankfully removed), which had seen action in France and weighed 30 tons in total. The tank arrived by rail at Frome railway station later in the year, and made the journey to the handing over ceremony under its own power with over 2,000 people lining the streets. According to local newspaper reports, the tank was presented to the town by Lieutenant McNab, who had driven it from the station to the recreation ground. In his speech he hoped that having been in such bloody action, the tank would now stand in 'the green and peaceful fields of Frome'. In the end, it enjoyed its tranquil surroundings for only twenty years before the neglected and rusting hulk was deemed an eyesore and sold off for scrap to the highest bidder - W Walter of Bath for £22/10- - proceeds given to the British Legion.

1923 The Great Fire of Cheap Street.
At around 10.45 pm on Saturday 4 August 1923 a fire broke out in the premises of Bailey's a draper's shop at numbers 9 and 10 Cheap Street. The shop was completely destroyed with flames reaching 30ft into the air and was described at the time as, 'probably the most disastrous fire in the history of the town'. The fire occurred in Frome's oldest street and the ancient wooden framed buildings burned with an intense heat.

The blazing timbers collapsed across the narrow street into number 17, the premises of Jack Dance's outfitter's shop and the fire raged as Mr and Mrs Dance slept upstairs and narrowly escaped with their lives by managing to get into a small yard at the back to escape the flames to be rescued by means of a rope being lowered down to them.

146 Looking Towards the Market Place

The fire hooter could be heard as far away as Beckington and raised the whole town with thousands clogging the narrow streets – so much so that they had to be pushed back by the police to allow the Frome Fire Brigade through - and it was only the swift action of the brigade that prevented the fire from spreading and causing casualties. Upon hearing that a small child was asleep in a building next door a Mr Benger dashed into the threatened and smoke filled room to rescue the child sustaining severe burns to his face and arms in the process.

So rapidly did the fire take hold that it was feared that the whole street might be consumed and even spread to King Street but gradually the

147 The Cheap Street Fighter Fighters

fire brigade gained control and by the early hours of Sunday the threat was contained. So grateful was the town for the prompt actions of the brigade that they presented the station with an ornamental lamp which was hung outside the fire station.

Of the buildings themselves Bailey's was rebuilt and is now the Hunting Raven bookshop. The badly damaged property next door at number 8 is Frome Wholefoods. Number 17 across the street is now Coiffure the hairdressers, and the old Flora tearooms next door, once the Albion pub continued for many years as The Settle bakery and restaurant.

The cause of the fire was never discovered but is thought to have been an electrical fault.

148 The Local Fire Truck

1925 The Frome Builders Strike.
As 1925 dawned Frome's builders were far from happy. The previous year had seen a nationwide strike by building workers which began when 600,000 men

downed tools at midday on 6 July and were to stay out for seven weeks after several years of acrimonious battling between masters and men. First one side, then the other, would gain advantage, the outcome at a particular time usually depending upon the state of trade, and the demand for labour. In the early part of 1924 a slump gave employers the upper hand and a pay cut of 20% with an increase in working hours from 44 to 47 hours per week. After much toing and froing, the dispute was settled.

In Frome, however, the men felt that they had been short changed and that they were due an extra penny per hour under the terms of the national agreement which the local Master Builders Association was refusing to pay – even refusing to meet the men's representatives in conference to discuss the situation. The employers considered 'the present rate of wages sufficient' and could see no general dissatisfaction amongst the workforce. As a response to this, the men took part in a ballot of members organised by the National Federation of Building Trade Operatives and by an overwhelming vote of ten to one declared in favour of strike action.

149 The Builder's Strike

Their basic demands were 1 shilling and four pence halfpenny per hour for craftsmen, excepting painters, (obviously) who would get 1 shilling and 3 pence halfpenny; labourers were asking for one shilling and a halfpenny.

Reporting of the dispute was very sparse and it is difficult to follow the exact sequence of events but it looks like the men struck on 21 February. The response was patchy with the men working for Seward & Son coming out as did those building the new Town Hall but those working for the same firm on other sites did not. Towards the end of the month over 100 men were involved but there is no figure recorded for the total walkout.

In mid-March the two sides agreed to talk and a joint conference was organised by the Ministry of Labour Conciliation Board. The men asked for one half penny now and another on 1 May but the employers would grant only the first part of the demand and talks broke down. The two sides met again towards the end of March and at last a settlement was reached after almost five weeks. The top trades were to receive an additional half penny per hour making their wages 1 shilling and 4 pence, and after July they were to gain an extra half pence. Painters were to receive 1 shilling and 3 pence halfpenny, labourers a shilling and a halfpenny per hour – pretty much what they wanted in the first place. There was no mention of the number of hours that the men were expected to work so maybe there was a compromise in that regard.

The accompanying illustration is one of the few to show the Temperance Hall, at the top of Catherine Street finished in 1875 and demolished in the 1960s it is now another car park.

1931 Buried at the Crossroads.
During the summer of 1931 some workmen were engaged in widening the road on the small triangle of land at the top of North Parade where Fromefield and Berkley Road divide. At the depth of about two feet they came across a human skeleton fully stretched out and buried face down. They contacted Rev. Arnold Cook who was the minister at Rook Lane Chapel and lived a short distance away at 33 Fromefield but by the time he arrived the site had been heavily disturbed and some of the bones had already been dumped.

Cook gathered up what he could which was most of the skull and some long bones and after consulting the police, who declared the bones to be ancient and not of interest to them he popped them in the post to the Somerset Archaeological & Natural History Society in Taunton where they reached the desk of its curator Henry St.George Gray. Gray was somewhat at a loss as to what to do with this unexpected gift so he parcelled them up once more and sent them to his friend Sir Arthur Keith at the Royal College of Surgeons. Keith was one of the country's foremost anthropologists and his confusing opinion was that, 'The size of the bones favour a Saxon burial but I think the remains are those of a Romano Britain.'

Gray had enclosed a ninepenny stamp so that the bones could be returned to Cook and there the matter could have ended – except that the reasoning behind Keith's conclusion, that the remains were from the Roman period, would not be accepted today without further evidence and Keith was one of the leading advocates of the fraudulent Piltdown skull being genuine. There was another possibility which does not seem to have been considered at the time.

Suicide was one of the most heinous crimes in the Christian lexicon but gave the church the problem of how to punish someone who was already dead and they arrived at an ingenious solution. A suicide would be tried by a coroner's jury of twelve local people and for the suicide to have been a crime the deceased had to have been of sound mind and to have understood what they were doing. An alternative verdict was that the death had occurred while they were mentally ill or disturbed in which case no blame was attached and the event was treated pretty much as an accident.

150 Junction of Berkley Road and Fromefield

If 'self murder' was the verdict the corpse was treated with a form of religious barbarism. Instead of a normal burial in a churchyard or consecrated ground with a service and mourners, suicides were buried by the roadside at night, sometimes at the crossroads but not always. A wooden stake was driven through the body and into the ground to prevent the resurrection of the offender on the day of judgement, either physically or symbolically. No prayers and no mourners, the grave was unmarked, and their very existence forgotten, - the very antithesis of a Christian burial.

The irony in all this is that the suicide often had their place of burial named after them and sometimes even a pub, especially if buried at a crossroads! This was unofficial of course but once the locals started using the burial to refer to a particular spot it was only a matter of time before the name appeared on a map and became adopted. Immortality was denied by church and state but the names of these unfortunate people have lived on long after those that condemned them. These macabre rites were abolished by the Burial of Suicide Act of 1823 which forbade roadside burials.

The best known example is of course Tucker's Grave at Faulkland where suicide Edward Tucker was buried at the crossroads in 1747. Another example could be Hellikar's Grave at the junction of Whitewell Road and Marston Lane. The name goes back to at least 1694 but nothing else is known. A card maker named Samuel Laverton hanged himself at The Trooper pub in what is now Trinity Street in 1764 and was ordered to be buried at the cross roads and John Adams hanged himself in the stable of a pub called The Crooked Fish in Frome in 1753. He was ordered 'to be buried in the common highway and to have a stake drove through his body'.

Could the skeleton at North Hill have been one of these? Once the remains were returned to Rev. Cook the probability is that he had them reburied quietly in a local churchyard and the true story will never be known.

1931 The Skeleton in the Hat Box.
In October 1931 Miss Rosina Strudwick a milliner and ladies outfitter was having some work done to the front of her shop, The Hat Box on the corner of Cheap Street and King Street. The building is often described as the oldest in Frome and had been a butchers, grocers and travel agents before being gutted and absorbed into the Café La Strada in 2000.

As the workmen removed some plaster from a corner wall they discovered an ancient window frame concealed in its depths and as they took away more of the covering they were shocked to find the righthand section of a human jaw bone with four teeth still in excellent condition and a human hip bone! Also amongst the rubble were two coins from the reign of George I (1714-1727). Speculation was rife. Were the bones from an ancient murder? Part of some superstitious rite? Possibly, but the most likely explanation is that the remains were washed out from nearby St. John's churchyard when its walls collapsed in 1799 and 'numbers of dead bodies rolled forth' down the slope. We will never know the truth.

Miss Strudwick was to have an eventful year. Once her new plate glass windows had been installed they were subject to repeated attacks by being scratched and smeared with grease and candle wax. Blinds were also slashed. Things became so bad that Miss Strudwick and her landlord took to concealing themselves in the shop at night waiting to catch the culprit. Eventually they caught a Mr. Vincent in the act. Harry Vincent was a fellow trader who ran a jeweller's shop at the other end of Cheap Street who despite being caught red handed denied everything claiming that the grease came from a candle he was using to look for rats! He was convicted and fined £1 plus £1 and 1 shilling in compensation. He never explained his actions and continued to trade on the street for many years.

151 The Pepperpot c 1902

1932 Tragedy at Willow Vale.
The spring of 1932 was remarkable for the amount of rain that fell on the town causing widespread flooding with rivers swollen to an alarming extent. On Monday evening 2 May a group of schoolboys rushed excitedly from school down to Willow Vale to gasp in amazement at the raging torrent which had risen to within a foot of the road over the town bridge. The river had risen about eight feet in two hours and pretending to be shipwrecked sailors, the boys clambered on to a derelict stone structure bridging the river which had been part of the housing for the old water wheel.

Without warning the stone arch collapsed throwing five boys into the raging torrent. One of the lads, Dennis Moore aged 11 had the good fortune to be dragged by the current towards the bank and was rescued by his friends

Danny Johns and Leslie Alcock, who managed to grab his arm and pull him clear – almost falling into the river themselves.

Police constable Edgar Olpin, a good swimmer, took off his helmet, cape and cloak and threw himself into the water; he reached the middle of the stream but the situation was hopeless as the boys were swept away before he could reach them. Olpin was in serious danger of drowning when he had the presence of mind to shout to one of the onlookers on the bank to throw him the end of his cape by which means he was dragged to safety in an exhausted condition. The four boys were swept under the bridge in a matter of minutes but in that dark and confined space their position was hopeless.

152 Remains of the Old Town Mill 1930s

Dragging operations began immediately and continued until it was too dark and dangerous to see anything. Operations were resumed at daybreak on Tuesday and at about 6.15 the body of Stanley Edwards, aged nine of The Mint was found over a quarter of a mile from the bridge. At 9.30 Anthony Horsefield aged eleven of Oakfield Road was found at Low Water with his satchel still strapped to his back. Harold Moore, the fourth boy, of Selwood Road and brother to Dennis was found on the Friday morning. On the day of the tragedy it was his ninth birthday.

The search for the remaining boy, Charles Sharland, 12 of Woodland Road continued and his body was not found until over two weeks later on Thursday 19. The coroner recorded a verdict of 'Death by Misadventure'. The funeral of Stanley Edwards, the youngest victim, took place at Holy Trinity Church on the 9th and the church was filled with mourners and many floral tributes. PC Olpin received much praise for his actions and was personally decorated by the king in the New Year's Honour's List with the King's Police Medal for Gallantry.

1935 Mavis Tate MP - A Woman Ahead of her Time.

Mavis Tate was Frome's Member of Parliament for ten years between 1935 and 1945. Of the 25 different people to have represented the town since 1832, she is the only female. During her time as MP, she not only represented the rights of her constituency, but also women in general.

She chaired the 1941 Women's Power Committee and the following year the Equal Pay Campaign Committee. She was a pro-abortionist and advocated the arming of women during the invasion threat of 1940. Her beliefs did not go down well with the government at the time and she inflicted the only commons defeat on Churchill during the war years. So annoyed was he, it is said, he ordered another vote to ensure victory. Mavis married twice, and her second husband was Henry Tate (of Tate & Lyle). On the liberation of the death camps she was one of ten MPs – and the only female – to go and witness the horror of what had been discovered. Mavis Tate subsequently narrated Pathe News' harrowing footage, which shook a nation during the summer of 1945.Later that year, like Churchill, she lost her seat in the post-war election to Labour. She committed suicide in 1947, having become ill from the time she visited the camp.

153 Mavis Tate on Pathe News 1945

1939 Gaumont Cinema, Cork Street.

One of the few art deco buildings to be constructed in Frome, the Gaumont opened in 1939 with 1000 seats in a stadium plan replacing the previous Palace Theatre. It changed its name to the Classic in 1967 before being demolished in 1971 – despite local opposition - to be replaced by the bland 1970s brown

154 The Gaumont Cinema, Cork Street.

155 Spirited Opposition to its Demolition 1960s

brick building, as part of the Westway development, another cinema this time the Westway Cinema.

1942 Any Old Iron?

Throughout the dark days of the war people of Frome were asked to donate any salvageable metal through unwanted domestic objects, such as saucepans and frying pans. The more that was asked of them, the more they seemed willing to give, digging deeper and deeper into their resources as the war dragged on. In time, however, need greatly outstripped supply and so compulsory 'salvage' schemes were introduced, the most contentious of these being the removal of iron railings. By the end of 1942, Frome Town Council, through an advertisement in the local press, announced the impending removal of 'unnecessary railings, gates, and bollards etc.'

The scheme for collecting scrap metal had started early in the war and at first the sources had been bombed buildings, along with derelict mine machinery and the like. Gates and railings soon became identified as a valuable source of raw material for war weapons and so London's public squares and royal parks were first to be deprived of them. In February 1943, it was Frome's turn and a schedule of properties whose owners were ordered to relinquish their valuable metal was drawn up and the work begun in earnest. Heavy hammers were deemed the most practical solution – given the short supply of hacksaws, saw-frames and oxyacetylene gas – but this led to a great deal of criticism. Permanent damage was caused to walls and buildings throughout the town as ancient iron work was wrenched from its historic settings destroying the grace and beauty of many of the streets. New 'stump extractors' were extolled as reducing this possible destruction considerably but the result was tragic nonetheless.

156 The Trail of Destruction

From North Parade to Keyford, from Rodden to Christchurch, contractors extracted the railings and other metal accessories destined to become munitions or military hardware. It didn't all go according to plan for the workmen employed to remove the metalwork, however, as one incident on the corner of Blindhouse Lane proved. Despite the shortage, an oxyacetylene burner was being used on an ornamental gas lamp. Unfortunately, the supply had not been disconnected and a 'fountain of flame' erupted! No one was injured, but once all the work was completed, the town was altered forever, as despite assurances, the town was never returned to its former appearance.

The population of Frome was left with the belief they had contributed significantly to the war effort and their somewhat aesthetic sacrifice had not been in vain. But in the recent years, this 'significant contribution' has been cast into doubt, with rumours of tons of scrap metal and decorative ironwork being merely dumped in the Thames or used as ballast on ships as far away as Cape Town or Melbourne apparently accounting for some fine balcony rails as the type of metal was useless for munitions and the whole exercise merely a propaganda campaign. Whatever the truth, Frome not only lost a greatly missed asset but was left in numerous cases with metal stumps embedded or protruding from low walls which can still be seen today. A poem which appeared in a local newspaper around the time the work was being carried out perhaps sums up the philosophical long-term situation the best.

Cheer up! Good folk of Frome,
It's not the crack o' doom,
You've lost your railings;
And these have gone for righteous cause,
To right the wrong, to keep the laws,
With neither fear nor failings.

1945 VE Day.
The town celebrated the war's end in style 8 May being a national holiday after nearly six years of conflict. The Prime Minister's announcement that the war was over was relayed to a large crowd in the marketplace from Woodmancy's shop. Flight Sargeant Amos Clark of the Mediterranean Allied Air Force who

157 The Official Order

came from Frome was awarded the B.E.M. at the palace and an American GI played Tipperary on the trumpet. Public buildings were illuminated and 10,000 boisterous people thronged the town. Many street parties were held with dancing and singing in the streets carrying on until the early hours and 5,000 people attended a celebration in Victoria Park with fireworks and bonfires, sadly spoiled by rain.

Fourteen year old Audrey Millward of Rodden Farm recorded the event:

We had a holiday from school, went into Frome in the afternoon on bikes to see flags and listen to a service in St John's outside. Frome decorated with flags. At 7 we went to a thanksgiving service in church. About 11.30 we lit a huge bonfire top of Homeground (it was a cart-load of straw) The Hawkins came along, Jimmy Crees and Graham Gillard. There were flashes, fireworks, search lights, bonfires and flares during the night.

Uncle went into Frome Tuesday night, he said they were very drunk and standing on top of cars, etc. and the Americans threw money and chewing gum in the air for everyone to pick up. They took hold of Sam Minty because he was in police uniform and poured beer into his mouth and they brought out glasses of beer and broke the glasses against the cars and walls.

On Wednesday we went to market but there were no shops open. At 11 o'clock went to a service at St Johns in Frome. We went into Frome at about 10, watched the crowd in the Market Place singing and dancing, nobody was drunk as the pubs had sold out the night before. We saw the flood lighting. We went to bed both nights about one o'clock. We put a flag on the barn and on the cart house, 3 in the garden and 3 in the little garden by the yard.

1949 Scandal at the Abbey !! A Dangerous Liaison.

Beckington Abbey is a beautiful and historic mansion dating back to 1502 which in 1946 had new owners; Lieutenant-Commander Geoffrey Russell of the Royal Navy, his wife Noel and their daughter Miss Frances Prudence Russell aged 23. The war had been over for months and the two women were settling into the ancient abbey and renovating its interior while Captain Russell was in London. To help with this they had the assistance of some inmates from the White House, Prisoner of War Camp which was the old Mendip Lodge, just outside the town.

One of these young men was Klaus Barth a German parachutist whose job it was to whitewash the Abbey ceilings. He and Frances were immediately attracted to each other and after she had spent some time admiring his work on the ceilings, they fell in love. One day in January of 1947 Klaus failed to

158 Beckington Abbey

159 Miss Frances

return to the camp and seemed to have disappeared. After a while the authorities gave up the search and there the matter rested until two years later when in January 1949 the newly appointed housekeeper, Mrs Isabelle Voyles, was asked to produce two breakfasts and deliver them to the quarters of Mr and Mrs Gold and their baby daughter.

The door was answered by a man calling himself 'Nicolas Gold' whom she recognised immediately as the missing prisoner of war Klaus Barth! He and Frances had married under his adopted name of Gold in July of 1947 at Lymington Parish Church and produced a daughter whom they named Noel after her grandmother.

After Voyles spilled the beans the Abbey was raided and the family, including Captain Russell, appeared at Frome Magistrates court charged, 'That between January 1947 and January 1949 they did wilfully and knowingly harbour Klaus Barth whom they knew, or had reasonable grounds for believing, had acted in contravention of the Aliens Order (1920) by failing to register or furnish particulars of himself'. Frances appeared in the dock alongside her mother, father and husband with the baby on her knee and they were remanded on bail for a week but Herr Barth was kept in jail while the authorities considered further charges. As the car took the women away from the court the door burst open throwing mother and baby into the road where they rolled over several times but both were happily unhurt.

Despite claiming rather lamely in their defence that they had had no idea that 28 year old Barth was German - they had introduced him to friends and neighbours as an Irishman whose mother was a Danish princess, mother and daughter were convicted and fined £75 each. The Lieutenant Commander was acquitted as he had been away in London for much of the time and was able to claim that he had no idea what was going on.

In what seems like a remarkably generous gesture Barth was acquitted of all charges, although it did emerge that he was in danger of being deported to the Soviet occupied East Germany so perhaps the authorities took pity on him. Whatever their reasons he was released to his wife and daughter and allowed to remain in the country.

Beckington Abbey was sold, the Gold/Barth family moved to Guildford and there our knowledge would have ended were it not for a misunderstanding over a book in WH Smith's four years later. It seems that Frances who was now styling herself Baroness von Barth had mistakenly picked up a book with her handbag and left the shop without paying. She was kept in custody without her husband having been informed and had her title called into doubt which outraged the magistrates so much that they dismissed the charges and ordered an enquiry into the behaviour of those prosecuting. Baroness Barth died peacefully in her sleep at her home in Herefordshire in April 2008 leaving eight daughters and fourteen grandchildren. The abbey is now converted into three dwellings.

1958 Frome Society Founded.

In 1956 an exhibition of local history was held in Frome to illustrate how fast things were changing and raise the question of how to preserve and record the towns disappearing past. The classic aims, then as now, were outlined as, 'To promote and further interest in natural history, geology, archaeology, architecture, local history and kindred subjects; to complete and reserve local records on the subjects, and to foster preservation in Frome of anything deemed to be of special interest in these matters'. An inaugural meeting was held with quest speaker the renowned archaeologist Sir Leonard Woolley, and the society began its activities.

Today the society continues with its aims organising coach trips in the summer and lectures in the winter publishing books and papers on local history as well as an annual *Yearbook* of local research free to members. The society can be contacted at:

Frome Society for Local Study: 1 North Parade, Frome BA11 1AT 01373 454 611
info@fsls.org.uk   www.fsls.org.uk

1960s The Sack of Frome.
It may seem unbelievable today, but at one time local authorities thought nothing of demolishing huge swaths of historic buildings and landmarks in the name of progress. During the 1960s and early 1970s an orchestrated programme of slum clearances wrought havoc throughout towns up and down the country and Frome was no exception.

The most affected area in Frome was at Trinity, which consisted of row upon row, street after street of residential housing that dated from the town's cloth trade heyday. It was in the 1950s, in the prevailing mood of the time, Frome Urban District Council designated Trinity as a Housing Clearance Area that was 'ripe of redevelopment'. Thankfully, it was decided to undertake this act of historic vandalism in stages, beginning, perhaps unsurprisingly, with what became known as Trinity Phase 1. In 1960, the Government approved a Compulsory Purchase Order (CPO), paving the way for the clearance work, which would take place throughout the next few years.

This phase related to the area bounded by Selwood Road (which was to be realigned), Milk Street, Castle Street and Trinity Street. Among the places consigned to history during this phase included Broad Street and Bell Lane – the latter being where Cockey's original bell foundry had been established. By 1967, the area had been rebuilt and the following year another CPO allowed the second phase of destruction to begin, concentrating on the north-east region. This time around, those places lost to the bulldozer included Peter Street, Rosemary Lane and Duke Street. Before it was completed, however, public feeling towards this wholesale destruction of the past began to turn and the first rumblings of conservation could be heard. By the time Phase 3 was ready to progress, the 'Save Trinity' campaign was well and truly underway and the fight to reclaim the town's history established.

What helped to a large degree, was the realisation that the housing in Trinity was much older than originally thought and, due to circumstances elsewhere, unique. The area had been built between the 1670s and 1720s, at the height of Frome's prosperity through its cloth industry, to house its

160 The Sack of Frome 1968 (Frome Museum)

many workers and those of related industries. Other places which had had equivalent areas – such as London and Manchester – had long seen the houses demolished when profit outweighed their historic value.

Because Frome had missed out on any similar investment for such a long time, these houses had remained intact, albeit in an increasingly dilapidated state. With the knowledge of its historic value now fully understood, demolition plans were reversed, and restoration became the order of the day which was just as well, as the Trinity area is now recognised as the earliest remaining large area of industrial workers' housing in the whole of Britain. Thankfully, the houses saved within Phase 3 consisted the oldest part of the Trinity area and were thus those of the greatest historical significance. These residential dwellings within Trinity, were not the only historic buildings once at risk but saved from the bulldozer throughout this period. Others included the Blue House, Rook Lane Chapel, Sheppard's Barton, Sun Street Chapel and even the building that today houses the Frome Museum. How the landscape of Frome would have changed beyond recognition if developers and town planners had had their way, but thankfully common sense and people power prevailed. Today locals and visitors alike can wander around the streets of this historic town and savour at least part of its incredible and significantly important past.

1966 Frome Museum Opens.
Once the Frome Society was formed in 1958 the obvious next step was to

look for premises to establish a museum. The first attempt was at Church Steps leading into King Street on 26 May 1966. It was not the most suitable of buildings and there were some serious disputes with the landlord but it was a start. In the summer of 1977 thanks to society member and local benefactor Katharine Ashworth the society was given Wine Street House to use as it liked and the museum moved into it. A good distance from the town centre, this residential building was again unsuited to service as a museum and the museum moved to his present home taking over the old Literary Institution a natural home dating back to 1869 as previously described.

161 Frome Museum in 2022 (Facebook)

The museum has an extensive library and research facility including an online searchable database. It holds regular exhibitions and lectures. Its library is open to the public as below or by appointment.

> Frome Museum 1 North Parade, Frome BA11 1AT 01373 454 611
> info@fromeheritagemuseum.org   https://frome-heritage-museum.org
> Open Tuesdays-Saturdays 10.00-2.00 March to November or by appointment for research,

1968 Field Marshal Montgomery.

In June 1968, Frome welcomed back a bona fide war hero, who had last visited the town during the darkest days of World War II. The return visit of Field Marshal Viscount Montgomery – victor of El Alamein – was as guest of honour at a luncheon given by Frome printers Butler and Tanner Ltd. on the occasion of the publication of his book *A History of Warfare*, which the renowned firm had been responsible for printing. A tour of the firm's printing works at Adderwell was conducted before the acclaimed warrior was taken to the Portway Hotel for the honorary luncheon. During the event, Montgomery was presented with a hand-tooled copy of the new book by Butler and Tanner's managing director, Mr Joseph R Tanner. The choice of venue no doubt stirred up potent memories for the field marshal, as this had been his temporary headquarters twenty-eight years earlier.

162 The plaque on the former Portway Hotel

The story began with Dunkirk, in May 1940, when the British Expeditionary Force, which included Montgomery's 3rd Division, had been evacuated to England. Once returned to British soil, his battered and scattered division was to reform in Frome, where Montgomery had decided to base his headquarters at the Portway Hotel. Portway House had been built as a private home in the 18th century but was converted into a hotel in 1934, six years before the War Office and Montgomery requisitioned it. Although still a hotel in 1968 – during his return visit – the Portway closed in the late 1980s and according to the book *The Historic Inns of Frome* was converted into retirement flats. Back in 1940, and before Montgomery's re-equipped division could head back across the channel, France fell, and he was reassigned to the south coast. Once there, the Major-General, as he was ranked at that time, and his men began to prepare the coastal defences against an expected German invasion. A plaque to commemorate Montgomery's brief tenure in 1940 Frome, along with his wider war contribution, was unveiled in May 1947 on the outside wall of the hotel. This was designed by H.E. Stanton, a former headmaster of the Frome School of Art and Science and made by Frome Art Metal Workers

Guild.

1968 Never Mind the Weather.
In July 1968 Frome experienced one of the worst floods in living memory. The prolonged and torrential downpour, along with an intense thunderstorm, reached the town during the early evening of Wednesday 10 July. The River Frome broke its banks around 11.30pm and by the early hours of the next day, Willow Vale, Bridge Street and Market Place were impassable. Most of the shops in Market Place were completely flooded, including Boots, Briggs' shoe-shop, two butchers (Somerset's and Baxter's) and Woolworths. One shop owner, had even taken the precaution of calling in his entire staff and they worked through the night moving goods to a safer and drier place.

At Wallbridge, Marley Carpets suffered considerable damage to its stock, a machine suffered a short circuit, and several fish were discovered swimming

163 Local birdlife contemplates its good fortune during the flood

in the premises. In the same area, a car and caravan spent the night stranded in the flood waters, while another vehicle was swept away by the torrent and imbedded in the river bed. As awful as 1968 was in Frome, flooding had been a regular occurrence over the centuries. The river regularly overflowed until its course near the bridge was moved and flood prevention measures adopted around the turn of the 20th century. Even this, did not stop the severe floods continuing, and they recurred quite regularly.

Rain is not the only purveyor of inclement weather, of course, and Frome has had its fair share of snowfalls as well. During the extreme winter of 1963 snow blocked the three major roads in and out of the town, while fifteen years later, ten feet drifts and a jack-knifed lorry did so again. Although 1976 is remembered for its heat, the year opened with 85 mph winds that brought down numerous trees in Frome and virtually cut it off once more. But whatever the weather – rain, shine, snow or wind – Frome is a resilient place and, of course, without it, there would be one less major topic to discuss.

1973 Population of Frome was 16,000.

1978 Out of this World ?

In January of 1978 the Portway Hotel in Frome was once more the subject of press interest.

It was subjected to an unearthly experience when it hosted a day long exhibition on the subject of Unidentified Flying Objects. The exhibition included pictures supplied by the 'UFO Info Exchange at Trowbridge' and the first showing of colour slides of what were claimed to be UFOs taken by the Apollo astronauts. The event was one of a number of events timed to coincide with the publication of a local tourist brochure entitled *Frome is Flying Saucer Land*.

The origins of what was to become first a local and then a national sensation lay back in 1961 when residents of Warminster began hearing strange noises that seemed to come from the sky. This was followed by four witnesses seeing a UFO shoot across the heavens leaving a trail of sparks and over the coming months many more strange aerial events were reported in the area. Reports soon reached the attention of the national press and the strange occurrences became known as the 'Warminster THING'. Pigeons dropped from the sky, dormice and partridges lay on the ground stunned, cattle stampeded, car engines stopped and 'elderly, very young and nervous people' were reported as being scared and terrified of the strange noises and reports of unexplained objects in the sky.

In 1965 Hilda Hebdidge saw UFOs that were cigar-shaped, and covered in winking bright lights in various shades of gold and yellow. These were silent and stationary, with no beams or rays, high in the sky and gradually faded as she watched. In June, Patricia Phillips phoned Arthur Shuttlewood an ex Grenadier Guardsman, one time local councillor and reporter for the *Wiltshire Times* and the *Warminster Journal*. From the summer of 1965 'The Warminster Thing' had become his life's work. At first he professed to be the cynical old reporter who was not fazed by anything, but as the story picked up so did his interest and he began to feed stories to the national press. Hilda described a 'brightly glowing, cigar shaped object,' that remained motionless over the south of Warminster for almost half an hour. Shuttlewood sold this story to the News of the World. Later in the month Kathleen Penton saw an enormous shining Thing going along sideways in the sky from left to right. It glided quite

UFO expert Arthur Shuttlewood shows a copy of his book to Mr Michael Pawley (left), owner of the Portway Hotel, and others interested.

164 Arthur Shuttlewood at the Portway

slowly in front of the downs and seemed to have porthole windows which ran along the whole length of it lit up the colour of yellow flames in a coal fire. It was very much like a train carriage she claimed, with rounded ends to it and gently gliding sideways.

At the age of twelve the present author managed to persuade his aged grandfather to drive from the other side of Bristol, climb to the top of Cley Hill and spend an afternoon with assorted photographers, tourists and 'spiritual people' waiting for the aliens to make contact. They haven't yet…

Some years later and back on the proper side of Cley Hill, Shuttlewood was the guest speaker at the Portway Hotel exhibition. Arthur had begun to see strange objects himself and claimed that he had managed to signal to one of them with his torch claiming that 'They came down so low that I could see the dome!' Not long after, Arthur began to stretch the credulity of the most ardent believer when he claimed that the 'saucer people' had been contacting him by telephone! Not only that - the unearthly beings even told him which telephone box they were using!

As interest in his stories spread so did his fame and the next logical step was to write a book which he did in 1966 entitled *The Warminster Mystery* largely a rehash of his old newspaper articles but shortly followed by more outrageous revelations in, *Warnings from Flying Friends* and a number of others. Lecture tours, promotions and magazine articles followed. People who met him were greatly impressed by his charisma, dedication and rustic charm and his audience was divided between those who respected his sincerity and those who thought him a charlatan. Whichever view is taken he certainly attracted a following and nobody can deny that some very strange things occurred along the Somerset and Wiltshire border in the mid 1960s many of which remain unexplained to this day.

1987 When Joni came to Frome.
Over the years the town has been host to many well-known musicians who have either played its venues or recorded nearby. One of the latter was Canadian singer-songwriter Joni Mitchell – *Big Yellow Taxi, Both Sides Now, Woodstock* – who stayed in Frome for a time in the late 1980s.

While her fourth studio album, *Blue*, is often cited as one of her greatest, it is the thirteenth that connects her with this area. *Chalk Mark in a Rain Storm* was released in 1988 and recordings for several of the songs off the album took place the previous year in Bath and nearby Beckington. It was during this period that Joni and her then husband, Larry Klein, who co-produced the album with his wife, lived in a house within the town. An interview the

165 Joni Mitchell

nine-time Grammy award winner gave to promote the album mentions Frome and dates her sojourn here from January to mid-June 1987. The first track completed was a duet with Peter Gabriel, called *My Secret Place,* which was recorded at his home studio in Bath.

Other songs were then recorded at the sadly now demised Wool Hall Studio, in Beckington, located in the village's Church Street. As its name would suggest, it was originally a sixteenth century storage place for wool but was converted into a recording studio by pop group Tears For Fears who after recording their *Songs From The Big Chair* album, let the studio out for other artists to use and it was during this period Joni Mitchell recorded there.

Other artists who took advantage of the studio's facilities included Paul Weller, Van Morrison (who would later own it), Annie Lennox and The Pretenders. The Smiths recorded their final album, *Strangeways, Here We Come,* there and after they split up, it was also responsible for Morrissey's first solo one, *Viva Hate.* As for Joni, *Chalk Mark in a Rain Storm* would be Grammy nominated for 'Best Pop Vocal Performance, Female' but lose out to Tracy Chapman's *Fast Car.* Her marriage to Klein ended in 1994, during their making of the album *Turbulent Indigo,* and Joni went on to win a Grammy for Best Pop Album.

2009 Jenson Button – Man of Speed.

In October 2009 Frome-born Jenson Button won the Formula 1 Grand Prix World Championship to assure his place in sporting history. Not bad for a lad who failed his driving test on the first attempt by trying to squeeze his car through too narrow a gap! Jenson Alexander Lyons Button was born in Frome in 1980 and lived the early part of his life at Northcote Crescent, before moving with his father to Vobster. Education consisted of going to Vallis School and Frome College, but from around the age of seven the youngster's focus was firmly elsewhere. Starting out with karting, he soon progressed to car racing first in the British Formula Ford Championship and later, the British Formula 3 Championship.

His first Formula 1 season was in 2000, when he drove for the Williams team. Stints for Benetton, Renault, BAR and Honda followed in succeeding years. The 2009 Championship, saw him driving for Brawn GP in a car complete with a controversial diffuser design. This gave his team an early advantage over the others and allowed Jenson to win a record breaking six out of the first seven races of that season. By the time of the British Grand Prix other teams had fought back with their own reconfigured designs and Jenson's superiority came to a spectacular end. Although a string of bad results followed, he had created what turned out to be an unassailable lead going into the sixteenth and penultimate race on 18 October 2009. This was the Brazilian Grand Prix and although Jenson could only manage to finish in fifth place, it was enough to clinch the World Championship. He became famous

166 Jenson Button Bridge 2019

overnight and a string of accolades followed. Although runner-up to Ryan Giggs in BBC's Sports Personality of the Year, he was awarded the MBE.

Frome being the town it is, the way of honouring its newly world-famous son was a little more idiosyncratic, taking the form of the Jenson Button Bridge – designed for pedestrians – and Jenson Avenue, located on the outskirts of town, which has a 30mph speed limit. Nonetheless, it felt like the whole town turned out to welcome Jenson back in 2013 when he returned triumphantly to turn on the Christmas lights. The Market Place was turned into a temporary racetrack, along which Jenson drove his F1 car as far as Stony Street and then sped back off towards the Cheese & Grain. The noise was deafening, the doughnuts thrilling and his speech from the balcony of the George Hotel inspiring. Despite his rich and famous lifestyle, he remains at heart, it seems, the down to earth boy that rode his push bike around the streets of Frome while growing up. So, to paraphrase the old saying, Jenson Button may have left Frome, but Frome has never left Jenson Button.

2017 Foo Fighters Hit Frome!
One of the world's most famous rock bands graced Frome with a two and

167 The Legendary Cheese & Grain, Frome

a half hour secret gig on 24 February 2017 using the town as the location to announce that it was headlining the Pyramid Stage at the Glastonbury

Festival,(or the Pilton pop festival as the locals know it). The gig made up part of an elaborate publicity stunt which began when mysterious boarding cards arrived by recorded delivery at some fans' houses and carried the name of a fictional airline, Obelisk Airlines. Many quickly cottoned on that the destination of these cards, which read CAG, stood for the Cheese & Grain in Frome. Foo Fighters were formed in Seattle in 1994 initially as a one-man hard rock project by former Nirvana drummer Dave Grohl. Since then they have become one of the most admired bands on the rock scene. They played at the Cheese and Grain for a full two and a half hours to the delight of those who managed to gain entry.

BIBLIOGRAPHY

Adams, D. *Frome's Fallen Heroes* 2000
Barrett, C. *Somersetshire: Highways, Byways & Waterways* Bliss, Sands & Foster 1894
Belham, P. *The Making of Frome* 1985 FSLS free as a PDF on Frome Museum website
Belham, P. *Villages of the Frome Area* FSLS free as a PDF on Frome Museum website
Browne, G. *St Aldhelm: His life & Times* SPCK 1903
Bunn, T. *Answers to Enquiries Respecting Frome Selwood* Penny 1851
Bunn, T. *Experiences of a 19th Century Gentlemen* FSLS 2003
Cruse, J. *A Map of the Parish of Frome Selwood* FSLS 2023
Cuzner, S. *Handbook to Frome- Selwood* Cuzner 1866
Daniel, H. *The Blue House, Frome* pamphlet 2010
Davis, M. *Of Mounds and Men.* Prehistoric Barrows of the Frome Area FSLS 2020
Davis, M. *A Surfeit of Magnificence.* The Trials & Tribulations of Sir Thomas Champneys. Hob Nob 2020
Davis/Lassman *The Awful Killing of Sarah Watts* Pen & Sword 2018
Davis/Lassman *Foul Deeds & Suspicious Deaths in and around Frome* Pen & Sword 2018
Davis/Pitt *The Historic Inns of Frome* FSLS 2022
Edwards, A. *Shining a Light on the Prehistoric Habitation of Frome.* Privately Printed 2022
Frome Times. Local newspaper, various dates
Gathercole, C. *Frome Archaeological Assessment.* Somerset CC 2003
Gill, D. *Frome School Days* FSLS 1985 free as a PDF on Frome Museum website
Gill, D. *Bath Street* Privately printed 1990 free as a PDF on Frome Museum website
Goodall, R. *The Buildings of Frome.* FSLS 2013
Goodall, R. *The Industries of Frome.* FSLS 2009
Harray, K. *Leversedge & Patton. A Family History.* Privately Printed, New Zealand 2014
HMSO *Early Industrial Housing. The Trinity Area of Frome* 1981
Lassman, D. *Frome in the Great War.* Pen & Sword 2016
Lassman, D. *Frome at War* Pen & Sword 2020
McGarvie, M. *The Book of Frome* 5th ed FSLS 2013
McGarvie, M. *Frome Through the Ages* 1st ed FSLS 1982 free as a PDF on Frome Museum website

McGarvie, M. *Frome Street & Place Names* FSLS 2017
McGarvie, M. *Crime & Punishment in Regency Frome* FSLS 1984
Moorhead, S. *The Frome Hoard* British Museum 2110
Morrison, C. *Frome Unzipped, from Prehistory to Post Punk* Hobnob 2018
Moxley/Jenner. *A Report on the Future of the Trinity Area of Frome* 1977
Overend, E. *The Geology of the Frome Area* FSLS free as a PDF on Frome Museum website
Pickering, A. *The Witches of Selwood* Hob Nob 2021
Pickering / Kearley. *Secret Frome* Amberley 2019
Robinson, D *Frome Preserved: A Museum's History.* Reflective Hedgehog 2016
Various *Frome Yearbooks* 1986-2023 FSLS free in PDF format on Frome Society website

FURTHER RESEARCH AND INFORMATION

Frome Society (for Local Study) FSLS
1 North Parade, Frome BA11 1AT 01373 454 611
publications@fsls.org.uk
info@fsls.org.uk
web. fsls.org.uk

Frome Museum
1 North Parade, Frome BA11 1AT 01373 454 611
info@frome-heritage-museum.org
web. frome-heritage-museum.org
Open March to November or by arrangement

Discover Frome (Tourist Info)
Frome Library, Justice Lane BA11 1BE
web. discoverfrome.co.uk
01373 465 757

Taunton Heritage Centre
Brunel Way Norton Fitzwarren Taunton TA2 6SF
web. swheritage.org.uk
01823 278 805

Witham Friary History Society
colincourtfarm@gmail.com

Keyford Local History
keyfordlocalhistory@gmail.com

INDEX OF PEOPLE AND PLACES

Streets, buildings, etc are in Frome, and villages and minor places are in Somerset, unless otherwise located.

Abbott, Roger 60
Achilles, motor car 162
Adams, John 112, 175
Adderwell 13, 187
Airthry Castle, ship 134
Albany, theatre 165
Albion, pub 171
Alcock, Leslie 177
Aldhelm, St 41–2, 45–6, 56, 62-3,197
Alexander, Ian 77
Algar's Farm, St 35
Allen, Thomas 84
Alsbury, Colin 47, 133
Amesbury, Wilts 70
Ammerdown 117
Anchor, pub 57
Anchor Barton 63, 119
Andy's Micro pub 112
Antedragus 30
Apple Alley 66
Ashmolean Museum, Oxford 39
Ashworth, Katharine 187
Athelstan, king 42, 49
Aubrey, John 34
Australia 131, 155
Avery, Mr 76
Avon, River and Gorge 26, 30, 97
Axbridge 152

Babcock & Wilcox 163
Badcox 107, 124, 167
Badgers Hill 165
Bagendon, Glos 30
Bailey's, shop 170, 171
Baily, William 131
Ball, Billy 93
Ballard, Mr, silversmith 29
Barth, Klaus 182–4
Bath 29-31, 38-9, 64, 94-9, 101, 106, 134, 145, 169, 192-3

Bath, Marquis of 120, 122, 126
Bath Abbey 82
Bath Street 29, 57, 63, 66, 102, 109, 118-21, 124, 126-7, 142, 168
Bath stone 49
Batt, Mr 87
Baxter's, butchers 189
Beckington 111, 140, 170, 182–4, 192–3
Belgium 165
Belham, Peter 11, 43
Bell Inn 85, 120
Bell Lane 185
Bendle, Herbert Henry 73
Benetton 194
Benger, Mr 170
Bennet 49
Bennett, W J E 49, 150–1
Beorhtwine 51
Berkley 43
Berkley Road 173, 174
Bigot, Richard 43
Bird, Stephen 39
Bird, Mr 158
Blackboy, pub 78
Blacklands Field, Hemington 33–4
Blackwell Hall, London 95–6
Black's Head, pub 78
Blaise Castle, Bristol 30
Blue Boar, pub 88-91, 112, 130
Blue House (School) 90, 92-4, 109, 115, 186
Booth, William 159
Boots, shop 189
Box, Henry 103
Boyle, Rear Admiral 136
Boyle Cross (Fountain) 56–7, 136
Bradford on Avon 48, 76
Bradford University 18
Braikenridge, George 145
Brakspear, Harold 59
Brawn GP 194
Bridge House 53

Bridge Street 57, 99, 100, 145, 189
Bridgwater 131
Briggehous 53
Briggs', shoe shop 189
Bristol 30, 69, 85, 91, 94, 134, 145, 152, 192
Bristol University 50
Brithwine 51
Britten, George and Martha 153
Brixton Deverill, Wilts 38
Broad Street 185
Broadway 166–7
Brooke, Andrea 93
Browne, family 15
Brownes' Hole 15–6
Brownjohn's Mead 57
Brunel, Isambard K 148
Brunswick Place 151
Bruton 97, 117
Buckland Dinham 26, 93, 152–4, 160
Bulls Bridge 98
Bull's Hotel 164
Bumpas, John 118
Bunn, Thomas 101–2, 119-20, 123, 134, 142–5
Burgundy, Duke of 65
Burton, C 133
Burwalls, Bristol 30
Butler and Tanner 160, 164, 187–8
Butts Hill 162

Camerton 20
Canada, Canadian 134, 192
Cape Town, South Africa 181
Carlyle, Jane Welsh and Thomas 150
Castle Cary 151
Castle Street 165, 185
Catcote, William 93
Catherine Hill 119
Catherine Street 173
Catley, Aubrey 153
Cenwalh (Cenwealli) 41, 45
Chamberlain, A 15
Champneys, Thomas S M 21, 136–40
Chapman, pub landlord 85
Chapman, Tracy 193
Cheap Street 46, 56, 62, 66-7, 109, 146, 170-1, 175-6
Cheese & Grain 57, 90, 123, 195–6
Cheshire 115
Chessils Field 37
Christ Church 127, 131
Christchurch Street East and West 67, 101–2, 119, 127, 130, 145, 152, 163, 167, 181
Churchill, Winston 178

Cirencester, Glos 30, 43, 45, 48, 56
Clarence, Duke and Duchess 63–5
Clark, Amos 181
Clark, James 93
Claudius, emperor 30
Claudius Gothicus, emperor, 37
Clavey, Joseph 70
Clavey's Barton 70
Clements, Thomas 76
Cley Hill, Wilts 192
Clifton Down, Bristol 30
Clink 38
Clink Road 40
Cobbett, William 128–9, 160
Cockey, Edward and Lewis 124, 134–5, 185
Codford, Wilts 153
Coit Maur 41
Coleford 97
Collinson, John 24, 145
Colt-Hoare, Sir Richard 34
Combe Hay 34
Constantine, emperor 26, 37
Cook, Arnold 173, 175
Coombs, Richard 83
Cooperative Society 167
Corfield, Liz 166
Cork, Earl of 58–9, 90, 102-3, 136
Cork Street 85–6, 101, 123, 137-8, 178–9
Corsley, Wilts 153
Cottles Oak 98
Courthouse, The 89
Coventry Herald 117
Cranch, John 112
Cray, Henry 67
Crees, Jimmy 182
Crees, John 86, 91
Crisp, Dave 39
Crocker, Abraham 89-90, 109, 112–3, 115–6
Crocker, Edmund 127
Cromwell, Oliver 76-7
Crooked Fish, pub 77, 175
Crown Inn (Hotel) 138–9, 149
Crown and Thistle, pub 57
Cruse, Jeremiah 53, 62, 75, 78–9, 98, 106, 122
Culver Hill 63, 115

Daniel, W E 49, 142
Dartmoor 147–8
Defoe, Daniel 94
Deggan, Edward 152–3, 157
Dekker, Thomas 74-5
Devonport 131–2
Dobunni 30
Dodge's, furnishers 103

Doulting 46
Downes, Catherine 37
Druid Stones, Orchardleigh 19
Drury, William 79
Duke Street 185
Dunkirk, France 99, 188
Dunstan, abbot of Glastonbury 50
Dusautoy, Mr 142–3

Eadred, king 50
Eagle Inn 91, 152
Easthill 14
Edgell, Captain 138
Edgell's Lane 90
Edmund, king 50, 60
Edmundson's Electricity Co. 163
Edward the Confessor, king 54, 56
Edward I, king, 58
Edward IV, king 63, 65
Edwards, Andrew 13–4
Edwards, Stanley 177–8
Egbert, king 50
Egford 33, 53, 159
Elliot, James 155
Eric Bloodaxe, king 50
Ethelwulf, king 50

Fairfax, General Thomas 76
Farleigh Hungerford 37
Faulkland 175
Faustina, empress 37
Feltham Lane 13
Finden, W (John) 126
FitzBernard, Ralph 58
Flora tearooms 171
Flower de Luce, inn 102
Fordbury Water 26
Foscott, Fair Maids of 83–4
Fox Hills 24
Foxcote 83–4
France 46, 97, 99, 169, 188
French, David and Hester 71-2
Fromefield 16–8, 26, 40, 138, 151, 173–4

Gabriel, Peter 193
Gane, – 154
Gare Hill 54, 155
Garston 94, 135
Garston Lodge 158–9
Gaumont Cinema 178–9
Gentle Street 61–2, 67, 70–1
George I, king 175
George III, king 117
George Inn (Hotel) 56–7, 101, 119, 123, 131, 135, 137–40, 143, 149–50, 167, 195
Gibbet Hill 86
Giggs, Ryan 195
Gill, Derek 102, 142
Gillard, Graham 182
Glanvill, Joseph 79–82
Glastonbury 50, 195
Gloucester 64, 100
Gloucestershire 30, 100, 117
Goddard, Silas 88
Goold, Valentine 153
Gorehedge 67–8
Gray, Henry St George 21, 173
Gray's Inn 128
Gray's sawmill 164
Green, Thomas 142–3
Greene King, brewer 78
Greenland, Byard and Uriah 153
Gregory, Isaac 86, 91
Grohl, Dave 196
Grove Lane 75
Guildford 184
Guy, Nancy 93

Halifax 96
Halley, Edmond 115
Hampstead Heath, London 135
Hannaford, T R 148
Harding & Co. 163
Harold, king 54
Harris, Dr 168
Harvey, John 107
Harvey, Mr, pub landlord 88
Hassell, Wilfred 168
Hawkins, family 182
Heath, Robert 45
Hebdidge, Hilda 191
Hecks, cider 113
Hellikar's Grave 175
Hemington 33
Henrietta, queen 77
Henry I, king 56
Henry III, king 58
Henry VIII, king 56
Herefordshire 184
Hertfordshire 115
Heytesbury, Wilts 70
Highbridge 113
Hiscox, James 102–3
Hobbs & Sons, garage 163
Hodder & Sons, builders 163
Hoddinot, Richard 152
Hogarth, William 156
Holborn, London 70
Holburne Museum, Bath 30

Holloway, John 72
Honda 194
Horn Street, Nunney 29
Horner, J S H 145
Horner, Thomas 103, 109, 125, 143
Horningsham, Wilts 49
Horsefield, Anthony 177
Horsley, Glos 117
Horton, Mark 51
Howarth, George 64, 86–7, 130
Howarth, Ralph 130
Howarth, family 64, 131
Hughes, Thomas 108
Hull, Edward 168
Hunt, Robert 80
Hurd, Robert 91, 147
Hwicce 45
Hylton, Lord 59

Ilchester 125
Ine, king 41, 45
Italy 46
Iveleafe, William 83

James II, king 86

Keith, Sir Arthur 173–4
Kellow, William 79
Kells, William 79
Kelsey's, furniture shop 103
Kent 163
Keyford 43, 63, 65, 114, 122, 130, 162, 167, 181
Kid, Captain 84
Kilmersdon 27, 152
King Street 56, 62, 66, 88, 170, 175, 187
King's Head, inn 78
Kingsdown Hillfort, Kilmersdon, 27
Kingsway shopping precinct 89
Kingsweston, Bristol 30
Klein, Larry 192–3
Knapton, Charles 73
Kyppinge, William 93

Lacey, Theophilus 86
Ladd, John 79
Lamb & Fountain 112
Lambdin, Ceri 37
Lancashire 115
Lansdown, Bath 99
Lassman, David 11
Laverton, Samuel 175
Lawes, Jayne 34
Leeds 30, 96
Leigh, Colonel 34

Leigh-on-Mendip 35
Leland, John 43, 53, 69–70
Lennox, Annie 193
Leversedge, Edmund 58
Leversedge, William 93
Leversedge, family 58
Lewis, Jodie 18, 22
Leystone Close 17
Limpley Stoke, Wilts 98
Lincoln 124
Linton, William 108
Littledale, Joseph 132
London 37, 70, 74–5, 86, 95–7, 128, 133, 135, 142, 150, 152, 159–60, 180, 182, 184, 186
Longleat 37, 71, 74, 78–9, 84–5, 106, 120, 122
Lyme Regis, Dorset 84
Lymington, Hants 183

McGarvie, Michael 11, 40, 43, 54, 58, 60
McGuinness, Mike 44
McKinley, Jackie 17
McLeay, Alastair 147
McNab, Lieut 169
Maes Knoll 30
Maggs, William 91, 146–7
Maggs-Sparrow gang 146–7
Magnentius, emperor 37
Maildubh, monk 45
Mallam, Benjamin 154–5
Malmesbury, Wilts 45–6, 48
Manchester 129, 186
Market Hall 123
Market House 138
Market Place 56–7, 62, 66–7, 86, 89, 91–2, 101–2, 112, 118–9, 122–3, 136–8, 149, 160, 164, 167, 170, 181–2, 189, 195
Marley Carpets 189
Marston 43, 54, 59, 66
Marston Lane 175
Marston Road 75, 98
Masonic Hall 142
Maundrell, James 73
Maximillian, emperor 65
Meade, Richard 143
Meares, John 79
Melbourne, Australia 181
Melksham, Wilts 126
Mells 25–6, 35, 43, 96, 98, 109, 117, 143, 145
Mendip District Council 67
Mendip Hills, Mendips 16, 27, 31, 41, 43
Mendip Lodge 182
Mercedes 163

Merchant, Henry and Walter 78
Methodist Church 131
Mid(somer)-Norton 153
Milborne Port 116
Milk Street 165, 185
Millgrove, William 153–4
Millward, Audrey 182
Minnitt, Stephen 51
Minty, Sam 182
Mitchell, Joni 192–3
Mompesson, John 79
Monmouth, Duke of 63, 84–6, 101–2, 144
Montgomery, Field Marshal Bernard 187–8
Montréal, Canada 134
Moore, Dennis and Harold 176–7
Morrissey 193
Murtre Farm House 20
Murtry 97–8, 154
Murtry Hill 19

Naish, Mr 97
NatWest, bank 101
Neale, Daniel 98, 100
Nernst lamps 164
Nero, dog 150
Neville, Isabel and Richard 63
Newbury, fort 26
Newport, Mr 87
North Field 94
North Hill 111, 175
North Hill House 144
North Parade 102, 110, 124, 145, 173, 181
North Somerset Yeomanry 125
Northampton, Marquess of 145
Northcote Crescent 194
Northumbria 50
Norton Radstock 23
Norton St Philip 70, 84
Norway 50
Nunney 29, 33, 54, 76–7, 94, 96, 167

Oakfield Road 177
O'Kane, Jennie 21
Old Bath Arms 119, 142
Old Nunnery House 63
Oldfield 43
Oldham, Lancs 129
Olpin, Edgar 177–8
Orchardleigh 19, 54, 140
Oxford 39, 79, 148
Oxfordshire 51
Oxley, Mr 130–1

Paddington, London 150
Palmer Street 63, 102, 119, 135, 142

Parret, River 41
Parsons, Mr, surgeon 158
Paulet, Colonel 95
Paulton villa 37
Peel, Sir Robert 152
Penselwood 41
Penton, Kathleen 191
Peonnum (Penselwood) 41
Pepys, Samuel 80, 83–4
Phillips, – 75
Phillips, Patricia 191
Piccadilly, London 151
Pierce, T 84
Pikewell 63
Pilly (Willow) Vale 136
Piltdown skull 174
Pilton, festival 196
Plaguy House 74–5
Plantagenet, George 63
Plymouth 79
Poole 31, 38
Portland 167
Portugal 97
Portway 124, 154, 166, 188, 190–2
Prater, Richard, and family 76
Prescott, John 38–9
Prescott's Head, 38
Pulteney Bridge, Bath 124–5

Radstock 23–5, 97–8
Reinbald 56
Renault 194
Rhine, area 22
Richards, Mr 98
Ripon 50
Rodden 14, 19, 43, 54, 181
Rodden Farm 182
Roddenbury 28
Rode 21, 122, 145–7
Romaine, Charles 72
Rome 31, 38, 46
Rook Lane 119, 145, 173, 186
Rose, Richard 78
Rosemary Lane 185
Rossetti, Christina, and family 151–2
Rossetti School 151–2
Rowe, Elizabeth 145
Ruddock, James 88
Russell, Geoffrey 182–3

Salisbury 95
Salisbury Plain 41, 79
Saunders, Abraham 103
Scotland 86
Scott, James 84; and see Monmouth, Duke

Seaman 58, 102, 105
Seattle, USA 196
Sedgemoor, battle 86
Selwood, forest 13, 31, 41–2, 45, 80, 160, 177, 185
Selwood Hospital 141
Selwood Road 160, 177, 185
Seward & Son, builders 173
Sharland, Charles 177
Shawford 70
Sheffield 160
Sheppard, Byard 138
Sheppard, George 138, 142
Sheppard, John 142-4
Sheppard, Thomas 135, 137-40
Sheppard, William 138
Sheppard, family 16, 21, 43, 89
Sheppard's Barton 186
Shepton Mallet 91, 98, 100, 117
Sherborne, Dorset 45–6
Shuttlewood, Arthur 191–2
Simpson, – 96
Singer, John Webb 29, 124
Sinkins, John 145, 150
Skinner, John 19-21, 23–5, 32, 34–5, 37, 105
Smith, Robert 85–6
Smith, Francis 155
Smiths, The 193
Somerset's, butchers 189
Standerwick 57
Stanton, H E 188
Station, Fire 171
Station, Police 73, 89, 152-3
Station, Railway 79, 102, 168–9
Steven's Lane 115
Stevens, Richard 114
Stoke St Michael 15
Stokeleigh 30
Stoney Littleton 20, 22
Stony Street 63
Stourhead, Wilts 109
Strachey, John 19, 63
Strada, Café La 175
Stratton 117
Strickland, Charles 39
Strudwick, Rosina 175–6
Stuckey's, bank 123
Summerhayes, Mary 73
Summers, Superintendent 87
Surrey 128

Talbot, inn 103
Tate, Mavis 178
Taunton 17, 30, 39–40, 131, 155, 173
Tedbury Camp, Great Elm 26
Tedworth, Hants 79–80
Temple Field 37
Temple of Science 145
Tetbury, Glos 99
Tetricus, emperor 37
Thames, river 181
Thompson & Co. 162
Tornay 69
Trowbridge 86, 138, 190
Tucker, Edward 175
Tucker's Grave 175
Twenowe. John 69
Twynyho, anchorite 63, 65

Vallis, manor 58
Vallis School 194
Vallis Way 155
Van Gogh, Vincent 126
Van Morrison 193
Vicarage 105, 142–3
Vicarage Street (Vicarestret) 62, 69, 91
Victoria Hospital 168
Victoria Inn 163
Victoria Park 182
Vincent, Harry 176
Vobster 194
Von Barth, Frances (Baroness) 184
Voyles, Isabelle 183

Wadbury Camp, hillfort 26–7
Walker, Mr, numismatist 29–30
Wallbridge 77, 166, 189
Wallbridge House 145
Wanstrow 168
Warminster 37, 70, 84, 98, 129, 134, 153, 190–2
Warwick, Earl of 63–4
Watts, P C 88
Watts, Sarah 91, 147, 153
Way, John 155
Wayland, John 78
Wayland, Richard 76
Wedmore 113
Weller, Paul 193
Wellow 34
Wells 96, 105, 134
Wesley Close 101
Wessex 41, 50
Wessex Archaeology 17
West Indies 129
West Woodlands 35, 91, 147
Westbury 70, 148, 150
Westerham, Kent 163
Western Australia 155

Westminster 152
Westway Cinema 180
Weymouth 117, 150
Weymouth, Viscount 37, 71, 84, 106
Weymouth Road 141
Whaltey 54, 96, 98
Whatley Combe, Roman villa 33
Wheatley, W W 65, 145-6
Wheeler, Henry 155
White Swan, pub 107
White House 182
Whitewell Road 175
Whittard, Mr 117
Wickham, James 93, 144
Wilcox, Babcock & 163
Wilkins, Clive, 157
Wilkins, Roger 112-3
William I, king 54, 56
William III, king 96

William IV, king 123
Williams, motor racing 194
Wiltshire 38, 54, 69, 108–9, 192
Winchester 50
Wine Street 187
Witham Friary 30, 40
Woodlands, West 35, 91, 147
Woodmancy's, shop 181
Woolley, Sir Leonard 184
Woolverton 153
Woolworths, shop 189
Worcester, battle 76, 78
Workhouse 134, 141
Wyatt, James 120–1, 133
Wyattville, Sir Geoffrey 119

York, Duke of 84–5
Yorkshire 96
Young, John 78

www.ingramcontent.com/pod-product-compliance
Lightning Source LLC
Chambersburg PA
CBHW042137160426
43200CB00020B/2967